MAY
CAUSE
MIRACLES

ALSO BY GABRIELLE BERNSTEIN

Add More ~ing to Your Life

Spirit Junkie

GABRIELLE BERNSTEIN

HARMONY

BOOKS · NEW YORK

A 40-DAY GUIDEBOOK
OF SUBTLE SHIFTS FOR
RADICAL CHANGE AND
UNLIMITED HAPPINESS

MAY
CAUSE
MIRACLES

All rights reserved.
Published in the United States by Harmony Books, an imprint of the Crown
Publishing Group, a division of Random House LLC, a Penguin Random
House Company, New York.
www.crownpublishing.com

Harmony Books is a registered trademark and the Circle colophon is a trademark of Random House LLC.

Originally published in hardcover in the United States by Harmony Books,
an imprint of the Crown Publishing Group, a division of Random House
LLC, New York, in 2013.

Library of Congress Cataloging-in-Publication data is available upon request.

ISBN 978-0-307-98695-5
eBook ISBN 978-0-307-98694-8

Printed in the United States of America

Text design by Ellen Cipriano
Cover design by Michael Nagin
Cover photograph by Dan Hallman

10 9 8 7 6 5 4 3 2 1

First Paperback Edition

For my husband, Zach.

I honor your miraculous journey.

Contents

MAY CAUSE MIRACLES

Introduction

*Heaven on Earth is a choice you
must make, not a place you must find.*

—WAYNE DYER

Winter 2009 was a turning point in my career. I was in the process of trying to get a publishing deal for my first book, *Add More ~ing to Your Life: A Hip Guide to Happiness*. At this time the recession had us in a headlock. Fear and uncertainty were at an all-time high, news anchors reported on the ever-growing unemployment rates, and nearly every industry was negatively affected.

I remember sitting in my mother's kitchen telling my stepfather about my book concept. He tried his best to be as supportive as possible, but his fear of the recession was very strong. He responded, "This is a great concept, Gab, but don't forget that right now is a terrible time for the economy. It will be hard to sell a book." My response was confident and almost involuntary—words flooded out of my mouth. "Thank you for sharing," I said. "But I don't think that way because I believe in miracles." I felt empowered by these words and filled with faith regardless of the outside world's resistance. In that moment I witnessed my commitment to letting go of fear and recalibrated my faith in miracles.

Three months later I sold the book.

For the past seven years I've been working hard to keep my mind clear of fear and maintain my miracle mind-set. As a result of my dedication to miracles I have become a raconteur for love, inspiring audiences worldwide through my global speaking circuit, books, and social media. Today I live a miraculous life and am on a mission to help everyone do the same. My dedication to miracles got me to this groovy state. But I'll be straight-up with you: choosing loving thoughts over fearful delusions was a tough transition at first. It seems easy—who *doesn't* want to trade in fear for love? But giving up fear is like giving up sugar: they're both sneaky ingredients that hide out in almost everything. And just when you think you've got that craving under control, suddenly it rears its not-so-pretty head again. Therefore, releasing fearful patterns isn't for dabblers. It requires diligence and commitment. It requires you to become a full-on miracle worker.

One of the key components to my glass-half-full lifestyle is my dedication to *A Course in Miracles*, which teaches, "An untrained mind can accomplish nothing." Over the span of nearly forty years, the *Course*, a self-study metaphysical guide published by the Foundation for Inner Peace, has changed the lives of hundreds of thousands of people. It can be approached in whatever capacity works best for the individual, and in my experience studying the *Course* resulted in a full-blown mind cleanse, not to mention a superrockin' life.

As a student of the *Course* I've learned that to find real happiness we must be willing to look at our fears straight-on.

Throughout my practice I was guided to examine all my fears and investigate their root cause. For instance, upon looking at my fearful patterns with food, such as bingeing and obsessing over the next meal, I could understand that my compulsive overeating was a reaction to the childhood anxiety I'd picked up at the dinner table. At one time, my mother struggled with overeating. She turned to food to anesthetize her own inner turmoil. Her compulsive overeating affected me because I unconsciously picked up her anxious energy around the dinner table. This seemingly minor experience created a lot of anxiety for me when it came to eating. Unconsciously I took on my own fear around food. The fearful thought *There's never enough* became an internal dialogue that plagued me at every meal. I'd overeat and speed through meals. I never tasted my food. I never even enjoyed it. I lived in this torturous cycle for years until I became willing to look at the fear underneath my behavior. Once I looked at my fear, I understood that it was based on that false belief that there was never enough. I spent decades in fear of not having enough to eat. I'd chosen to carry that limiting belief into my present and replay it in my day-to-day life. And that's the thing about limiting beliefs. They're just smoke and mirrors, a bit of mental sleight of hand that leads us in the wrong direction in life. Through my willingness, dedication to miracles, and infinite patience I was guided to all the resources I needed for healing. In time, my food addiction lifted.

Upon realizing that overeating wouldn't ever make me feel safe and complete, I recognized that nothing outside of myself could fill me up. I learned that real happiness doesn't come from *getting* but from *giving*. I accepted that true serenity and happiness come from a connection to love. Deep down we all inherently want to love and be loved. When we fulfill our function, which is to truly love ourselves and share love with others, then true happiness sets in.

As soon as I made the *Course* part of my daily life, I cleaned up my fearful thought patterns. Everything began to change. The most significant change wasn't *what* I experienced, but instead *how* I experienced it. As a result of following the *Course's* suggestions, I've forgiven my past, released my future, and shown up for the present with love and faith. The changes in my life were beyond phenomenal.

Now I'm going to show you how to do the same.

How to Become a Miracle Worker

The first step in choosing love over fear is to understand your fear. As a student of *A Course in Miracles* I learned to become the witness to my fear-based thoughts. Each time I felt fear set in, I'd take a deep breath, step outside of my thoughts and actions, and witness my behavior. By witnessing my fears I saw how delusional they actually were. For instance, early in my career I ran a public relations business. Every new client brought a new opportunity to negotiate my monthly retainer. I hated negotiating. It made me feel anxious and jittery, and I'd lose my sense of calm. When I acknowledged my fears around negotiating for more money, I realized it was related to a fear that I'd acquired as a young woman: that women shouldn't ask for more. This was an outside projection the world had created and I'd chosen to believe it. I honestly don't even remember where or when I picked it up, but it stuck to me like glue. This fear-based illusion from the past replayed itself enough times that it became a belief system I was faithful to. But by getting honest about my fear, I determined how this lack mentality had become a fear-based pattern in my mind. Throughout the book, I'll reinforce the message that witnessing your fearful patterns is the first step to detaching from them, and I'll provide support and guidance as you witness your own fears in all areas of your life.

Then comes willingness. You can change a pattern only if you're willing to change it. A *Course in Miracles* says that the slightest willingness is all you need to receive the guidance to change. When we become open to letting go of our fear, we open our heart, mind, and energy to be guided to a new perspective. Willingness raises your consciousness of new possibilities and ignites what I call your ~*ing* (your inner guide). Your ~*ing* is the voice of love, your inspiration and your intuition. Your ~*ing* steers you out of fear and back to love. All you need is a little willingness to get your ~*ing* on and receive guidance to change.

This guidance will come in different forms: intuition, inspiration, and sometimes even through synchronicities. Often we can experience intuition as a strong inner knowing that offers us guidance of some form. Inspiration can be experienced as a feeling of flow and excitement that comes through in moments when our thoughts and actions are aligned with love. Then there are moments of synchronicity, which are really groovy— like when you're thinking about your mother and she calls or when you keep hearing about a new book and the next day it falls off the shelf in the store. As you add up the exercises in this book, the presence of your inner guide will become more apparent while intuition, inspiration, and synchronicity will flow naturally.

Three other components are key to living a miraculous life: gratitude, forgiveness, and love. First comes gratitude. An emphasis on gratitude is the only attitude for the miracle worker. Living a grateful life creates more abundance, acceptance, and appreciation. To transform your fears back to love, you must embrace a grateful way of being.

Then comes forgiveness. The act of forgiveness is to the miracle worker as lettuce is to the raw foodie. Forgiveness allows us to cleanse ourselves of the old, junky fear and shines light on the darkness of our worries, doubts, and suspicions. Rather than continuing to play the role of victim, we can forgive and be set free. With each choice to forgive, we shift our perception from fear to love.

Finally, there is love—the most crucial ingredient. A *Course in Miracles* teaches that the only thing missing in any situation is love, and where there is fear there is no love. Therefore, living with an open heart and embracing love as our true purpose is essential to living a miraculous life.

Experiencing Miracles

The payoff for sticking to the *Course* principles is that the more you choose gratitude, forgiveness, and love, the more miracles you experience. If you're wondering what I mean by "miracle," it's simple: a miracle is a shift in perspective from fear to love. A miracle can be the moment you choose to forgive your ex-lover and let go of decades of resentment, or the moment you recognize that losing your job was not a tragedy but an opportunity to follow your true calling. Simply put, each moment you choose love over fear is a miracle. And the more miracles you add up, the less likely you are to perceive life through dark-colored lenses. When you choose to perceive love over fear, life begins to flow. You feel peaceful and you see love in all situations. Your hang-ups subside and your life feels guided.

My dedication to living this way has changed every area of my life. I've let go of addictions to romance, drugs, work, food—you name it. I've learned to choose forgiveness whenever resentment creeps into my mind. Fear of financial insecurity has lifted and my internal abundance, my zest for living a love-guided life, is reflected in external abundance. Today I see obstacles as opportunities and know that the Universe has my back. Most important, I feel a sense of certainty that there is a power greater than me supporting my every move. My ~ing is on!

When you release your fears, you too will begin to raise your thoughts and therefore your energetic state. Your body is a molecular structure that is always vibrating energy. That energy is positive when your thoughts are positive, and it is negative when your thoughts are negative. Our energy fields are like magnets; they attract their likeness. Therefore, if your energy is negative . . . guess what? You're attracting negativity into your life. For instance, if you walk into a job interview thinking you're not good enough for the position, you energetically exude insecurity and a sense of inadequacy. This energy is not attractive to the employer and you don't get the job. In this instance your thoughts informed your energy, and your energy negatively affected your reality. The miracle-minded approach shows you how to shift your thoughts and energy, thereby attracting positivity into your life. Had you walked into the job believing you were good enough, your energy would exude that same strength.

Then the positive impression you made could lead to immediate employment or a future connection. Either way, your positive energy will create a positive result. Releasing fear requires honesty and courage—but it's simple. And if you're willing, you'll be able.

Want to achieve these groovy results? Join me on the journey of new perceptions.

The Forty-Day Miracle Worker Commitment

Like any effective practice, true transformation occurs with daily repetition. Begin with a forty-day commitment and start experiencing positive results immediately. Why forty days? Metaphysicians and yogis place much emphasis on the repetition of a forty-day practice. Mythical examples range from Moses's forty days and forty nights spent on Mount Sinai to the story of the Buddha reaching enlightenment on the full moon in May after meditating and fasting under the bodhi tree for forty days. The number has scientific significance, too: research has shown that after repeating a new pattern for forty days, you can change the neural pathways in your brain to create long-lasting change. So let's take a cue from the mystics and scientists and commit to this forty-day fear cleanse. (Because this practice takes place over six weeks, you'll actually have forty-two days for the fear cleanse, an extra two days to practice our miracle work!) It's the simple, consistent shifts that count when you're making change—so I've outlined this journey to be fun and achievable. I will guide you to keep it uncomplicated and stay on track. And one day at a time you'll become a miracle worker.

By choosing to follow this plan for the next six weeks, you'll begin to reprogram your thoughts from fear to love. If you dig the results, stick to the path and commit to a life as a miracle worker.

This book is divided into six chapters, one for each week. The weekly chapters contain exercises for each day of the week to transform your thoughts back to love. Each week focuses on a different area of your life:

- **Week One.** This week guides you to identify how fear has tripped you up and blocked your life's flow. I'll lay the groundwork and guide you to embrace the key principles: witnessing your fear, willingness to change, shifts in perception, gratitude, forgiveness, expecting miracles, and reflecting and recapping.

- **Week Two.** This week is all about the importance of self-love. You'll be guided to strengthen your relationship with yourself, and you'll become willing to release old patterns of self-attack. Self-love is supercrucial to the miracle-worker practice.

- **Week Three.** I'll give you practical exercises that shift your patterns of self-sabotage when it comes to food and your body. I will guide you to identify the root cause of your food and body issues and begin to shine light on any darkness in this area of your life. You'll quickly come to realize that ingesting loving thoughts greatly enhances how you ingest your food and perceive your body.

- **Week Four.** Romance is in the air! I'll help you get honest about how fear has held you back from romantic bliss. This week incorporates many of the *Course*'s rockin' teachings for releasing fear in romance. These powerful tools will lead you to experience immediate internal shifts around romance, whether you're single or attached.

- **Week Five.** I'll guide you to focus on how fear has blocked your financial abundance. This week's exercises activate gratitude for your current workplace, help you address your financial fears, and guide you to shift your limiting belief system around money and work. This week is applicable to any type of work, whether you're a freelancer, a stay-at-home mom, a philanthropist, a banker, a salesperson, and so on. Just apply the principles to whatever work you do.
- **Week Six.** You'll learn to embrace the practice of being a miracle worker in the world. This week helps you shift your focus from yourself to your power to create energetic change in the world around you. Service is a key principle in *A Course in Miracles* and is strongly emphasized this week. You'll come to realize that serving the world is like serving yourself a big, heaping plate of love. When you focus your thoughts and energy lovingly on others, your heart opens and your true purpose shines bright.

Each week builds upon the next, layering exercises and strengthening your mental muscles as you embrace the miracles. Each day incorporates the same outline to create repetition within your daily routine and in your mind. As you repeat these practices, they'll become easier and easier until they become second nature. Though you may experience some bumps along the way, making the shift can be easy if you want it. When you're willing to change, you're given all the energy and support you need to move forward. Commit to each exercise and expect miracles!

How It Works

This book is meant to be a guide for you to create subtle shifts for miraculous change. Therefore, don't get hung up about the process. If you follow the simple daily steps, you'll be hooked up with all you need. Try your best not to skip ahead or practice more than one exercise a day. Each lesson is artfully placed right where it needs to be. Do your best to stick to the plan— but if you feel that you need to stay on a specific day for a little while, that's totally cool. Feel free to repeat days if you need to go deeper into the exercises. But trust ultimately that there is a plan that is well crafted for you. Each exercise will create subtle shifts. These shifts are miracles. And the more miracles you add up, the more miraculous your life will be.

Before you start exercising your love muscles, it's important that you prep for your journey. So next are a few things you'll need to know and prepare before starting your journey.

Prepare to Meditate

A superneat part of this book is that many of the exercises are self-reflective and very calming. I'll guide you throughout each day to establish and deepen your own meditation practice. Each exercise has written guided meditations that are also available bundled together as an audio album on my website, www.gabbyb.tv/meditate.

Your Meditation Space

To heighten your self-reflective experience, I suggest you set up a meditation space in your home. Maybe it's a corner in your bedroom, a nook in your office, or simply the edge of your bed. Find a space where you can be alone and feel at peace. My meditation space at home has a meditation chair (as seen on my website www.gabbyb.tv/meditate), candles, incense, Post-its with positive affirmations, and inspirational images and quotes. Most important, it is a space where I feel centered and calm. You will use your meditation space for your morning and evening exercises. This space will become sacred to you. It's likely that it will become your favorite place to hang.

Your Journal

In addition to your meditation space, you'll need a journal. You may want to have it with you throughout the day to document your shifts, so make sure it's small enough to toss in your bag.

Self-Care

Throughout your miraculous transformation you may feel overwhelming emotions. This is a good sign, trust me. But if you're not making self-care a priority, your emotional breakthroughs can morph into meltdowns. So make sure to activate specific self-care activities throughout each day. For instance, I love lighting a candle and taking a bath. The simple exercise of taking a bath is an act of self-care that supports me throughout all kinds of shifts. Regardless of what's going on, my daily bath is essential. So pick one or two acts of self-care that you will incorporate into your practice. You may want to be extra conscious to eat healthful foods, drink more water, or sleep more. Know that this is a transformational course that will crack you wide open. Be prepared to keep yourself in balance by consciously paying attention to self-care. Eat well, sleep well, think well.

Be Aware

Throughout your journey, remain mindful that fear is tricky. Right when you think you've got the love thing down, fear will sneak back in. This is nothing to be afraid of—just be aware. Being conscious of your fear behavior helps keep it in check. Also, since you'll be working your self-care so well, your fear will have less room to creep up. Love will take up so much space in your mind that fear won't have anywhere to go but out. Trust this and know that love will always shine brighter than fear.

Getting Down to Business

Now that I've laid the groundwork for your miracle-minded process, it's time for you to set your schedule. I suggest you begin the exercises on a Sunday. Each new week begins by reading the upcoming week's introduction. So this coming Sunday, read the introduction for Week One and start Day One on

Monday. You don't have to stick to this routine, but test-drive my suggestion and see if it works with your schedule. This process isn't meant to be rigid; rather, it offers you guidance to create your own transformational practice.

Take this practice seriously. Trust that as you change your thoughts, your actions and experiences will change accordingly. As *A Course in Miracles* says, "You may believe that you are responsible for what you do, but not for what you think. The truth is that you are responsible for what you think, because it is only at this level that you can exercise choice. What you do comes from what you think." Each day of the practice you will be guided to "exercise the choice" to change the way you think. As you add up new perceptual shifts you will begin to see miraculous changes throughout your life.

Now it's time to let go, be guided, and expect miracles.

WEEK 1

BECOMING
MIRACLE
MINDED

*My thoughts are images
that I have made.*

—A Course in Miracles

Fear: False Evidence Appearing Real.

Yup, that's right: when you focus on fear, it becomes your reality. We've all picked up fear in unique ways and replay these fearful stories over and over like mental movies in our minds. Each fearful belief we hold is a choice we make. We choose to believe in the fear on the news, the fear in our home, and the fear in our mind. Fear is an epidemic. Throughout our lives we absorb fear from the world around us, and we grow to believe those fears are our reality. Each of us in some way has chosen to hold on to fear in one or many corners of our life. Maybe you're fearful of not having enough money, maybe you're afraid to be alone . . . or maybe you're just straight-up fearful of everything. That was the case for me.

For more than two decades I lived in fear. I feared not being smart enough, pretty enough, or cool enough as well as not having enough. I even feared being too great. Fear ran the show. Each waking moment of my life I worked hard to anesthetize my fear with food, romance, love, work, drugs, gossip, television— anything to avoid actually dealing with my fear. I replayed my fear-based thoughts like a skipping record. I lived in a constant state of anxiety and inner turmoil.

Then when I was twenty-five, I hit a big bottom. Fear had sucked the lifeblood out of me. I was emotionally, physically, spiritually bankrupt, and addicted to drugs—I had no other choice but to find a better way to live. I had to surrender to a faithful voice within that had been calling my name for years. On the evening of October 2, 2005, I said a prayer for the willingness to see things differently. I prayed for love to enter into my fear-based mind. And it did. The next morning, an authoritative inner voice of love came forward and encouraged me to change my perspective on living. My inner voice said, "Get clean and you will live a life beyond your wildest dreams." My willingness to follow that message helped me to hear my intuition and reconnect with love. I've been listening ever since.

That decision has been the key to living with a miracle mind-set. I was willing on October 2, 2005, and then again on October 3, 4, 5, and so on. I'm still willing today. My deep desire to see love instead of fear is what got me here. Just as my inner guide had promised, today I am living a life beyond my wildest dreams. I am the happiest person I know, and I owe this happiness to one simple choice: love.

In every situation, no matter how horrifying it may be, we have a choice: the choice to see love instead of fear. I know this is a pretty far-out statement coming from someone whose darkest hour included drug addiction and deep inner turmoil. Yes, plenty of people throughout the world have experienced far more horrifying fears than what I've known, but we share one thing in common: we all have the choice to perceive love instead. We can choose to focus on the fear in front of us or open our hearts and surrender to a power greater than ourselves to restore our faith in love.

Throughout the book I'll refer to this "greater power" as an ever-present energy of love that circles around us, supports us, and guides us to know peace. Call it God, call it ~ing (inner guide), call it spirit—for the sake of this book let's call it *love*, although I'll use those words interchangeably.

Don't confuse this with romantic love; rather, consider it a presence of inner power that can attract more power to it. It's as if we have a magnetic force within us. When we clear the fear that blocks our power, then we become a magnet for miracles. The exercises throughout the book will guide you to release the fear that stands in the way of your connection to this loving power. A *Course in Miracles* says, "Your task is not to seek for love, but merely to seek and find all of the barriers within yourself that you have built against it." Yup, that's right, you don't have to go hunting for this awesome love—the power of love is already within you. But unfortunately events happen in our lives that become like bricks in a wall. Each fear-based experience adds another brick to the wall that blocks you from your inner power. My job is to give you the tools to dismantle these bricks to release all that separates you from your loving, powerful truth.

The "barriers within yourself" that have blocked you from your loving perspective are founded on the fear-based projections of what A *Course in Miracles* calls "the ego." The ego is synonymous with fear and produces judgment, attack, jealousy, and all the negativity that separates you from your loving truth. The ego is the opposite of the presence of love within us. We all have chosen to hook into our own ego perceptions in different ways based on our own experiences. One person's ego projects fear of financial insecurity whereas another person's ego projects poor health. The story your ego has told you may seem unique to you, but know that you're not alone. Everyone in this world (except for a few enlightened masters) experiences his or her ego on a daily basis. One of the primary tools for releasing the ego is to become highly conscious of its behavior. A major theme throughout this book will be to witness your ego in action. By placing the magnifying glass on your ego's dark illusions, you weaken its strength.

Understanding the Ego

A *Course in Miracles* teaches that when we choose our ego's false perceptions, we become separated from God (a.k.a. love). All it took was one tiny mad idea to make us choose the fear of the world over love. In an instant we can pick up a tiny mad idea from the world. For instance, I picked up the tiny mad idea that "there's never enough" from my early childhood mealtime experiences. In some way or another we all pick up the fear-based beliefs from our early childhood experiences. From that point forward we've continued to detour into fear and choose the ego's illusory perspective over our loving truth. The moment we chose fear over love our mind split off into what the *Course* refers to as "the wrong mind." Our right-minded side thrives on peace and oneness, but our wrong-minded side is fueled by the fears of the world. Over time the repetition of our ego's fear leads us to believe that the wrong mind is all there is.

The ego cannot survive without fear. Therefore, it's committed to keeping us stuck in fear with its crafty tricks. Outlined next are some examples of how the ego holds us back, keeps us small, and blocks our inner state of love.

Sin, Guilt, and Fear

When we side with the ego and believe that we've separated from love, we unconsciously feel as though we've sinned. This belief in sin creates an experience of guilt. We feel this unconscious guilt because we think we've killed our connection to love. Then comes the inevitable fear, the emotion we experience based on the thought that we need to be punished for turning our back on love. To keep us in this sin/guilt/fear struggle, the ego convinces us to deny the experience of fear to keep us stuck in the pattern. We deny our fear in all sorts of situations; for example, the drug addict is unwilling to admit his or her addiction, a woman makes excuses for her abusive spouse, or, more subtly, someone simply hates his or her job but is too afraid to walk away. The ego has crafty tricks for keeping us stuck in fear-based experiences that clearly do not serve us. When we're unwilling to look at our fear head-on, we accept fear as our reality. To further deny our fear we project it onto others in hopes that the guilt will magically disappear by placing it outside ourselves. Placing blame on others is a sure sign we're unwilling to look at our own deep-rooted fears. This is a sneaky ego trick that merely reinforces our faith in attack, judgment, and negativity.

I know all this must sound totally trippy. That is to be expected. Your ego has worked hard to deny your sin, guilt, and fear. Becoming aware of your sin/guilt/fear cycle is the first step toward changing it.

Separation

From a spiritual perspective we are all connected energetically. The *Course* says, "There are no private thoughts." This means that on some level we are all energetically connected through our shared intentions. The *Course* emphasizes our interconnectedness, that we are all one—black, white, male, female, poor, rich, and so on. Accepting our oneness helps us release the ego-based projections we have placed on the world. Unfortunately, most of us have not been taught to believe in oneness. We believe in the ego's false perceptions; we believe we are separate from everyone else. We see our bodies as more special or less special than others. Each thought we have reinforces our separateness and specialness, thoughts like: *I have more money that that guy*, or *I will never look good enough to get the romantic partner I desire*, or *I'm not good enough to be friends with you*. And on and on the ego goes. Each fear-based thought deepens the illusion of separation.

Judgment and Attack

The ego is the great faultfinder. Because our choice to perceive fear has made us feel so terrible, we project that terrible feeling onto others to "protect" ourselves from actually dealing with the discomfort. For instance, I spent years feeling as though I was incomplete without a romantic partner. Each time I'd see a happy couple I'd attack their romance in my mind by judging their relationship. I'd think thoughts like *That will never last* or *He can't possibly like her, can he?* Rather than choose to recognize their love as a mirror to the love within me, I chose to deepen the separation with judgment and attack. This is a fierce ego trick that keeps the illusion of separation alive and kicking.

Each week I will help you become more and more clear of how the ego uses its nasty tricks to keep you stuck in fear. Focusing on the ego will help you see it as separate from your loving, miracle-minded truth. The more you witness the ego in action, the less power it has over you.

The Way Out of the Ego

In addition to looking directly at your ego, you'll also be guided to surrender your ego fears to a power greater than you: your inner guide (a.k.a. ~ing). This inner guide is the voice of love, an internal teacher, waiting for our call. The *Course* says, "Love will immediately enter in to any mind that truly wants it." When we turn our fear over to this inner voice of love, we're offered powerful, creative ways of perceiving our life. For instance, if you turn your financial fears over to the care of your inner guide, you will be led to find new and unique ways for earning rather than staying focused on your lack. Or if you surrender your cigarette addiction to the care of your inner guide, you'll intuitively be guided to books, people, and resources that will help you recover from your addiction. Surrendering your fears to your ~ing will always offer you a miraculous solution.

Each exercise in this book guides you to create subtle shifts for miraculous change. The shifts occur when you choose to surrender your fear to your inner guidance system for healing.

A *Course in Miracles* teaches that prayer is the medium of miracles. When you release your fears through prayer, meditation, affirmations, and the daily unique practices throughout this book, you'll be guided to transform those fears into love. This book strives to make surrendering your fear a moment-to-moment habit. Through your willingness to choose gratitude, forgiveness, and a new perspective you will intuitively be led to see your entire life through new lenses. The more you call on love, the more love you will see.

I know that the concept of working with your inner power may be foreign to you. That's where this week's work comes in handy. Each daily practice this week will strengthen your mental and emotional love muscles so they become superstrong. But as I've stressed before, it takes time and commitment. It's just like working out: for the first couple days you feel a little out of whack, but as you get stronger and more fit, the whole process starts to feel natural (and awesome).

Remember: the key element to accessing the power of love is to believe in the power of love. One of my spiritual mentors, Wayne Dyer, some years back added a new twist to an old saying. He said: "I'll see it when I believe it." The goal of this book is to help you heighten your miracle-minded belief system so that miracles become your reality.

Each daily exercise this week will introduce the recurring principles that will show up throughout your forty-two-day practice:

- **Day 1** you'll begin the practice of witnessing. I'll guide you to witness your fears so that you can start to understand the choice you've made to focus on them.

- On **Day 2**, you'll be guided to surrender to the willingness to change. This may sound hard, but trust that you're already halfway there. Just by picking up this book you've made a major statement to yourself that you're willing to see love instead of fear.
- On **Day 3**, you'll begin to choose a loving perspective and start to say no to fear.
- **Day 4** focuses on gratitude, which will awaken the love presence within you and give you some extra juice for Day 5's heavy lifting.
- The work on **Day 5** is dedicated to forgiveness. Don't freak out—I'm not expecting you to forgive everyone in an instant. This week I'm simply introducing the possibility of forgiveness to ignite your willingness to jump-start the practice of the F word.
- On **Day 6** you'll be guided to awaken your miracle mind-set of love. I'll lead you in exercises that will help you step outside your comfort zone to see a world beyond what you have previously chosen to believe in.
- On **Day 7**, I'll conclude the week's exercises with self-reflection and preparation. You'll spend the last day of each week reflecting on the previous six days. Then, in the evening, you'll prepare for the week to come by reading the introduction to the next chapter.

Got all that? Simple right? Now that you're clear about the plan, I can share this week's promise with you. As you awaken your love mind-set, you'll begin to know a new truth:

1. Being miracle minded will enhance every area of your life.
2. You'll come to understand your fear and therefore be willing to release it.
3. Each exercise offers up a subtle shift in your perspective toward life. The more subtle shifts you add up, the more peace you will feel.
4. Judgment, attack, and anger will subside.
5. You'll inherently know a new serenity, and miracles will occur naturally.

Pretty amazing stuff, huh? Clearly, you have a lot to look forward to! Remember to focus on each exercise, be patient, and breathe deeply along the way.

Now let's get the ball rolling and bust through some fear.

Day 1

WITNESS YOUR FEAR

Welcome to your new life! Today we begin a journey of new perceptions, an adventure that will change the way you experience everything. Your goal today is to be the witness of your thoughts, actions, and energy. Up to this point it's likely that fear has been running the show, and you might not have even been aware of it. Maybe you've been avoiding asking for a raise because you're afraid of rejection. Or possibly you're afraid to follow your passion because you believe you'll have to give up financial security to do so.

When we're not aware of our fear, it takes residence in every area of our lives.

Today's work is to raise your consciousness and open your mind to your fear-based patterns. You must witness your behavior if you want to truly change it. You must look at your fear head-on to recognize that believing its lies was a choice you made. Today you'll begin a journey of choosing differently.

Everyone has individual fears that are unique to them. Each of us picks up fear from our past and re-creates it in the present, then projects it onto the future. Each day we make the decision to forget about happiness and choose to project fear onto our "reality." Today's practice will help you become mindful of how you've been committed to your fears. A *Course in Miracles* teaches that projection is perception—therefore, whatever fear-based beliefs you've been projecting onto your internal movie screen have become the film that is your life. It's time to become conscious of what you've been projecting so that you can begin to rewrite the script.

■ Morning Reflection DAY 1

Begin your practice today by reading the following morning reflection. Immediately following the passage, sit for one minute of silence—close your eyes and breathe deeply in your nose and out your mouth. This minute of silence will let the message set in and permeate your being. Remember that the work we do together will be subtle. Therefore, you may not think one minute of stillness will have an effect, but trust that every second you choose a new perspective is a miracle.

> *Today I am the witness to my fear. I open my heart and mind to see how I have chosen fear over love. Today I will watch myself as if I'm standing across the street peeking into the world I have created. I will witness how my fears run the show. I will pay attention to my patterns. Without judgment I will become conscious of where my mind chose wrongly and how these fear-based thoughts have tainted my happiness. I know*

this practice is the first step to uncovering my destructive patterns to create powerful change. I am ready, willing, and able to look at the delusional thoughts I've been projecting. I'm willing to witness my fear.

Affirmation Day 1

I AM WILLING TO WITNESS MY FEAR.

Whenever you notice your fears rise up during the day, repeat the preceding affirmation. For instance, if you become anxious at work, nervous before a date, or uncomfortable meeting someone new, you can simply use your affirmation: *I am willing to witness my fear.* The practice of witnessing your fear is important because it guides you to understand your triggers. This awareness will be helpful in upcoming exercises.

Take this message with you throughout the day by plugging it into your phone as an hourly reminder. When the alarm goes off, read your affirmation to gently remind yourself to look courageously at your fear straight-on and say, "I am willing to witness my fear."

Miracle Moment

In addition to using your affirmation, set your alarm on your phone for noon (or your lunch break) with a notification called "miracle break." This is your Miracle Moment, and trust me, it has the power to shift the energy of your whole day! When your alarm buzzes, gently remind yourself to choose love over fear by reciting your affirmation.

■ Evening Exercise **DAY 1**

Once you're home from your workday, take ten minutes to reflect on what came up for you. Take out your journal and
reflect on your day. Write down your answers to the following
questions:

1. What experiences trigger my fear?
2. What thoughts trigger my fear?
3. What are the feelings that come over me when I am
   in fear?
4. How does my fear affect my behavior?

Throughout the next six weeks, you'll use your journal to
document your process. Each journal entry will act as a bench-
mark for your progress. Be sure to take this step seriously, because we'll be reflecting on your work in later weeks. If writing
down your feelings is unfamiliar or challenging, don't sweat it!
Just put pen to paper and do your best to answer the questions
and let your thoughts flow. Over time, it will become easier and
you'll notice the impact of writing down your answers.

Now make a list of the fears you have uncovered. If the
exact fear is clear to you, then simply write it out. Be mindful,
though, that you may be unable to pinpoint your fear head-on.
If this is the case, then it may actually be easier to become
aware of the ways you may be "playing small," that is, hiding
out or avoiding certain situations. For instance, maybe you
skipped the gym again. Is it possible that you're nervous about
the way people will look at you? Or maybe you didn't speak up

in the office meeting. Could it be that you have a deep-rooted fear of your ideas being rejected? By paying close attention to your behavior, you can begin to get honest about what fears you may have been denying.

Once you've identified a few of your fears, take a moment to determine which fears are the strongest. Choose your top three fears and then rate each one's strength on a scale of 1–10 (10 being the strongest). Write these fears at the top of a new page in your journal and repeat your affirmation out loud: "I'm willing to witness my fear, I am proud of myself for doing this work."

When you're ready to retire for the night, prepare for another exercise. Each night I will guide you into self-reflection, work that opens up your subconscious mind so that your practical mind can take the backseat. Let go of your to-do lists and clear space for inspiration to come forth. This evening I'll guide you in a meditation that will help you reflect on the day with a loving perspective. Today's work may have brought up some uncomfortable stuff. That's cool. Remember that facing our fears is a huge part of this practice—after all, if we don't witness the fear, we cannot be set free from it. In this meditation, I'll guide you to energetically disconnect from the fears that have been present today.

The upcoming exercise is your first meditation. Follow my guidance below, or visit www.gabbyb.tv/meditate for the audio meditation.

In your meditation space, sit up straight on the floor or on a chair. Gently allow your shoulders to fall into a natural position. Get your body into alignment to receive the energetic guidance that will come through your meditation.

Close your eyes and place your hands on your knees, palms

facing up. Take a deep breath in through your nose and exhale out through your mouth. Continue this cycle of breath as you center into your meditation.

- Take a moment to reflect on the fears from your day.

- Allow yourself to become present.

- Center into your body.

- Breathe deeply in through your nose and out through your mouth.

- Continue this cycle of breath.

- Breathe in the feelings that came up for you today.

- Allow yourself to honor any feelings of discomfort, anxiety, or fear.

- Be present with your feelings.

- Breathe in your feelings.

- Exhale and release.

- Honor and allow yourself to accept whatever feeling is with you now.

- Take one last deep breath in and release.

- When you're ready, open your eyes to the room.

Day 2

BECOME WILLING

Today's practice is crucial to living with a miracle mind-set. The slightest willingness to see your life with love will be the catalyst for your greatest change. When you become willing to change, you surrender to a greater perception, a loving perception. That full surrender reactivates the communication to your ~ing (inner guide). The loving voice of your ~ing will become more and more present the more often you surrender to it. Today's work is about letting go and surrendering to the deep desire within. When you let go, your surrender will crack open your connection to your inner guide—and the loving voice that comes forth will lead the way to new perceptions and become an everlasting companion throughout your miraculous transformation.

■ Morning Reflection **DAY 2**

To kick off Day 2, let's move into the following morning reflection. Immediately after reading the passage, sit for one minute of silence—close your eyes and breathe deeply in through your nose and out your mouth. Let the words settle in and create subtle shifts.

> *Today I am willing to see things differently. Today I am willing to change my mind. I know a simple shift in perception will create a miraculous shift. I know change is what I need. I surrender, I am willing, I am ready to see love. ~ing, show me what you've got. Show me the way . . .*

Affirmation Day 2

I AM WILLING TO SEE THIS DIFFERENTLY.
I AM WILLING TO SEE LOVE.

Let this affirmation guide you out of fear every moment you feel stuck. Use it to open your heart and surrender to love.

It's time again to set your midday alarm with your Miracle Moment. Today's Miracle Moment is a reminder to be willing. When your alarm buzzes, recite your affirmation, *I am willing to see this differently. I am willing to see love.*

■ Evening Exercise **DAY 2**

I am willing to see love instead of this . . .

Today's evening exercise is a very powerful tool. Heads-up: you may resist this practice at first. What I'm about to ask you to do is a little mind-blowing. But that rocks, because blowing fear out of your mind is exactly what you need.

Let's get started.

Take a moment to reflect on your day, and make a list of all the fears that came up for you today. Next to each fear write this affirmation from *A Course in Miracles*: "I am willing to see love instead of this." For instance, if your fear was, "I'm afraid to speak up in the office meeting for fear of having my ideas rejected," simply write: *I am willing to see love instead of this.*

Make your list of fears and then affirm that you're *willing to see love instead.*

Today's practice of willingness is slight but powerful. Before bed, let's go deeper with your willingness—we'll activate your practice of surrender in a major way. Allow me to be your guide with the following. For the audio meditation, visit www.gabbyb .tv/meditate.

- Get comfortable in your meditation space.
- Sit up straight and take a deep breath in through your nose and exhale out through your mouth.
- Continue this cycle of breath throughout the meditation.
- Use this simple mantra as your guide.

- Breathe in: *I choose to release my fear.*

- Breathe out: *I surrender.*

- Breathe in: *I choose to release my fear.*

- Breathe out: *I surrender.*

- Breathe in: *I choose to release my fear.*

- Breathe out: *I surrender.*

- Continue breathing in and out this mantra until you're ready to open your eyes.

Day 3

CHOOSE A NEW PERSPECTIVE

For the past two days you've become the witness to your fear and opened up the willingness to release it. The third step is to choose to see love instead—so today's work introduces the practice of proactively choosing a better perception. The exercise of flipping your fear upside down is an awesome tool that we'll use throughout the book. For now we'll keep it simple (but still very powerful). I'll guide you to stretch beyond your limiting beliefs by choosing a more positive perspective. Continue to surrender to my guidance and have faith in love. Remember, you no longer need to figure it out . . . I've got your back! Now let's work together to transform your fear.

■ Morning Reflection DAY 3

Let's begin another daily practice by reading the morning reflection. Immediately following the passage sit for one minute of silence—close your eyes and breathe deeply in your nose and out your mouth. Let the words settle in and open your heart and mind to new perceptions and new ideas.

> *There's always a loving perspective. Today I welcome new perceptions. I am willing to let go of my old limiting beliefs and let love enter in. I choose to believe that there is always a loving perspective. I choose to see love.*

Affirmation Day 3

LOVE DID NOT CREATE THIS.

This message from *A Course in Miracles* is a powerful reminder that fear is an illusion and only love is real. Bring this affirmation to your fearful illusions, and in the moment remember the falseness of your fear. On Day 2 you were guided to become willing to see love instead of fear, and today you're affirming that love did not create your fear. These exercises build upon one another, strengthening your commitment to love. Use this affirmation throughout the day whenever you witness fear sneak in. You don't need to intellectualize the process. Just respond to your fear with this loving affirmation and let your ~*ing* do her thing.

Before you head out the door, make sure to set your midday Miracle Moment with today's affirmation: *Love did not create this.*

At some point today take an inventory of how your affirmation is affecting your experience. Write down one moment in which you used your affirmation this morning, and then answer the following questions:

1. What was my fear?
2. How did it feel to use my affirmation?
3. How did my energy shift (if only for a moment)?

■ Evening Exercise **DAY 3**

I once tweeted the affirmation "I choose to see love instead of this." And one of my Twitter followers responded: "Easy to say but not easy to do . . ." My initial reaction was *Man, that Twitter sister needs to open up to miracles.* But I understood where she was coming from. That used to be me, and unfortunately she's not alone. Our fear-based minds believe that change is tough and self-reflective work is difficult. But let's face it: being consumed by fear is far more difficult than showing up for love— we're just tricked into thinking fear is "easier" because it's more familiar. When people at my lectures complain that change takes too much time and energy, my response is, "It takes a lot of time and energy to feel like crap, right?"

With that in mind, tonight's evening reflection strengthens your commitment through writing a letter to your ~*ing* and surrendering to love even more. Take out a pen and a piece of paper, and write the following:

> *Dear Inner Guide,*
>
> *I am committed to transforming my fears to love. I will open my heart and mind to love and I will let my intuition guide me. I welcome all the spiritual assignments that may come and I am ready, willing, and able to smother my fears with the light of love. I choose to see love instead of fear.*

Sign the letter and post this letter on your desk, your bathroom mirror, or a vision board—somewhere that you can see it often. Post it in a sacred space that is just for you.

Day 4

GRATITUDE IS THE ATTITUDE

The fourth day of every week is really awesome, because it's focused on gratitude. When we are grateful for what we have, we raise our energetic vibration. Then our higher-level energy attracts more high-level experiences to create a domino effect of love. Gratitude is an integral part of the miracle mindset and will have a profound impact on your energy.

Throughout this practice you will be led to heighten your awareness of gratitude. The fear voice of your ego will resist gratitude at all costs. The ego loves to seek problems and focus on what we don't have. Understanding your ego's resistance will help you as you build your gratitude muscles and unleash your appreciation. Trust that the feeling of gratitude is stronger than fear.

■ Morning Reflection DAY 4

Let's begin today's practice with a powerful morning reflection. Take a moment to read the following passage and then sit in stillness for one minute. Let the feeling of gratitude come over you. Focusing on the feeling of gratitude, even for just a moment, will reactivate your loving energy field. This energy is what you need to support the flow of your transformation. So be willing to feel the greatness that gratitude has to offer.

I begin my day with gratitude. I am grateful for another day. I am grateful to breathe the air. I'm grateful for the trees, the grass, and the sky. I open my mind to focus on gratitude today. I release all littleness, all limiting beliefs. I choose gratitude instead.

Affirmation Day 4

GRATITUDE IS MY ONLY ATTITUDE TODAY.

Set yourself up with daily reminders to focus on the good stuff. Gratitude unleashes the loving presence within you and will awaken your miracle mind. Focusing on gratitude reconnects us with love. Throughout the day, turn to your affirmation as a gentle reminder to let go of your fears and focus on gratitude instead.

It's time again to set your midday alarm with your Miracle Moment. When your alarm goes off, recite your affirmation.

■ Evening Exercise **DAY 4**

Begin this evening's work with a gratitude list. Break out your notebook once again. Take a moment to write down a list of ten things in your life that you're grateful for. They can be big or small—whatever it is you're grateful for today.

Now let's go even deeper. This evening is an opportunity to see gratitude in the difficult areas of your life. It's easy to be grateful for the good stuff, but it's a whole other thing to be grateful for the difficult areas of life.

Begin by revisiting your notes from Day 1, when you identified your fears. Then make a list of your top five fears, and then next to each one write what you've learned and why you're grateful for these assignments. Take a moment and try to see your fears in a new light. Couldn't these difficult situations in your life be offering you opportunities for growth? The answer is YES! This exercise helps you to focus on how your fear is guiding you to grow rather than to stay stuck. So, for instance, maybe noticing your fear in relationships is calling you to deal with a deep feeling of loneliness you experienced as a teenager or after a bad breakup. Maybe there's a hurt there that never got the proper treatment or time to heal. Or maybe your issues with your family members have brought all the negativity to the surface so that you can deal with it now. Rather than look at your fears as problems, be grateful for the loving assignment for spiritual growth. All problems offer us opportunities to strengthen our faith in love. It may be difficult to see that opportunity in some problems—but be willing to see growth opportunities in all difficult situations.

Day 5

THE F WORD—LEARNING TO FORGIVE

Forgiveness is the bedrock of a life filled with love and miracles. Practicing forgiveness allows us to let go of our old fear-based past and center into the present moment. Through forgiveness we can release resentments that we may have held on to for decades or ones that just formed. The fifth day of each week will be focused on forgiveness.

If we remain unforgiving, we block the voice of love. A *Course in Miracles* says: "The unforgiving mind is full of fear, and offers love no room to be itself; no place where it can spread its wings in peace and soar above the turmoil of the world. The unforgiving mind is sad, without the hope of respite and release from pain. It suffers and abides in misery, peering about in darkness, seeing not, yet certain of the danger lurking there."

To break through the suffering, darkness, and misery that unforgiveness creates, we must take this step seriously. Today's practice is crucial. We begin the practice of self-forgiveness. That's right: we're starting with YOU!

■ Morning Reflection **DAY 5**

We begin this day by releasing self-hatred and self-attack through the practice of forgiveness. Let's begin the process of changing your inner dialogue toward yourself. If you're someone who loves to beat yourself up, diminish your accomplishments, or judge yourself for every action, then this step is for you! Get comfortable in your meditation space and read the following passage. Then sit in one minute of stillness and let the release of forgiveness come over you.

> *Today I let myself off the hook. I look upon my life's experience with a loving eye. I forgive myself for all my fearful thoughts and actions. I know that when I let go of my anger and self-attack I will recalibrate my loving presence within. I forgive myself and clear space for loving guidance to set in. Today, self-forgiveness is my primary function.*

Affirmation Day 5

**I FORGIVE MYSELF FOR CHOOSING FEAR.
TODAY I CHOOSE LOVE INSTEAD.**

Today's affirmation reiterates your willingness to forgive yourself. We can sometimes be hard on ourselves for having chosen fear for so long, but the truth is, we often didn't know any better. Now that you've committed to the way of love, you'll learn to forgive yourself for choosing fear—and begin to choose love instead.

Before you head out the door, make sure to set your midday Miracle Moment to remind you to recite today's affirmation: *I forgive myself for choosing fear. Today I choose love instead.*

■ Evening Exercise **DAY 5**

Forgive the projections you have placed upon yourself. A *Course in Miracles* teaches that what we project, we perceive: what we see inwardly determines what we see outside our mind. This exercise will call out your ego's projections and shine light on them with a loving response. Take out your journal and list five ways you've projected fear onto yourself. Then, next to each fear, respond with love.

For example, consider this fear and possible response:

Fear: I will never find true happiness.
Loving response: This fear is not serving me. I forgive this fear and choose love instead.

This exercise may seem uncomfortable at first—that's normal and totally cool. Stepping outside your comfort zone is exactly what you need. Remember that this work is not about staying stuck—instead, the work guides you to face your fears head-on so that they can transform through your daily practice. Trust that your desire to forgive will unleash a presence of peace throughout your being.

To disconnect from your faith in fear, the *Course* guides you to forgive everyone and everything—including your fear. When you forgive your fear, you acknowledge that it isn't real. Through forgiveness you can perceive fear as a wrong choice you have projected rather than believing it to be the truth. Forgiveness reminds us of our loving state. When we reconnect with love, we remember that fear is not real. This evening's practice will help you begin the process of forgiving the fear-based projections you've placed upon yourself.

Wrap Your Fears with Love

Before you go to sleep, open your notebook and write a letter of forgiveness to yourself. In this letter, revisit all the fears you've projected onto yourself. Look without judgment at what you've been projecting and perceiving to be real. When you open the letter, acknowledge the ego's fear and use your affirmation from Day 2, *I am willing to see this differently. I am willing to see love.* Let this affirmation reinstate your faith in love. As you continue writing, bring in more love. Reiterate your willingness to see love instead. By the end of the letter, begin to wrap your fears with love and compassion. In this conclusion, remind yourself that you've been doing the best you can. Honor yourself for showing up for your happiness. Then close out with a final message of love. Self-forgiveness will be a huge part of your practice in the coming weeks, so stay open and willing to grow in this way.

Day 6

EXPECT MIRACLES

Early in my recovery from fear I found it hard to believe that miracles were available to me. I was stuck in fear and limitations, and the thought of a miracle was so far from what I knew and thought about every day.

What I learned as a student of *A Course in Miracles* is that a miracle is simply a shift in perception. The moment we choose to let go of fear and choose love instead, a miracle occurs. The *Course* teaches, "Miracles are natural. When they do not occur, something has gone wrong."

If you're missing miracles in your life, what's that "something" that has gone wrong? The answer is simple: You have become faithful to fear. The moment our mind detours into fear, we cut off communication with the loving voice within us and block the miracle. Even though there is miraculous loving energy supporting us at all times, we're not aware of it when we're stuck in fear. Therefore, as you commit to your miracle mind, it's so important that you frequently remind yourself that miracles occur naturally. Today's practice will guide you to open your mind and reignite a mustard seed of hope that miracles are available to you now.

■ Morning Reflection DAY 6

Let's begin today's practice with a morning reflection that will help you jump-start your miracle mind-set. Sit comfortably in your meditation space and read the next passage. Then sit in stillness for one minute and let the words set in.

> *I forgive myself for getting stuck in fear. I believe in miracles. Today I am grateful because I have the willingness to remember that miracles are my birthright. Today I open my consciousness and participate in the cocreation of miracles. I know that when I am miracle minded, I have the capacity to witness and experience miracles in all corners of my life. I believe in miracles.*

Affirmation Day 6

I BELIEVE IN MIRACLES.

This simple, four-word affirmation is endlessly powerful. Say it out loud for extra oomph and witness the shift in your energy. If you feel silly or awkward at first, remember that a miracle is simply a shift in perception from fear to love. Plug this affirmation into your phone or computer calendar and get in the groove.

I suggest you set this Miracle Moment every hour on the hour. What a nice way to go through the day, right? Hourly reminders to believe in miracles! Enjoy the guidance.

■ Evening Exercise **DAY 6**

Take a moment to reflect on your day and become aware of when you were blocking love by focusing on fear. Remember that when you block your loving perspective with fear, you cut off your connection to miracles. (Yup, it seems nuts to cut off our connection to miracles, but most people do it all the time by turning to fear instead of love.)

Take out your notebook and highlight one moment during the day when you blocked love. Maybe you were rude to someone on the street, snapped at a coworker, or woke up with a bad attitude and carried it around throughout the day. Jot down one instance in which fear took over.

Reflecting on that negative moment may bring you back into that negative state. For a minute let yourself simply feel the negativity that comes over you. Once you're ready, say out loud to yourself, "I forgive myself for getting stuck in this fear. I know there is a loving way to see this. I believe in miracles." Then sit in stillness for one more minute and let the energy of these words settle into your emotional body. Give yourself the time to let love step in and take the wheel. Breathe into the feeling of relief that comes through when you affirm your faith in miracles. Notice how your body relaxes and your forehead softens. Pay attention to the miracle and savor it.

Tonight let's end the day with an inner guidance meditation. The work you've done this week has opened you up to connect to a power greater than yourself. In this evening's meditation, I will guide you to begin communicating with your own inner guidance system of love. Visit www.gabbyb.tv/meditate to download the audio meditation.

INNER GUIDE MEDITATION

- Sit comfortably in your meditation space.

- Place your palms facing upward and take a deep breath in through your nose and breathe out through your mouth.

- Continue this cycle of breath throughout your meditation, deeply breathing in your nose and out your mouth.

- Set the intention in your mind to clear the blocks to the presence of miracles in your life.

- Breathe in: *Inner Guide, thank you for guiding me to new perceptions.*

- Breathe out: *I am willing to see love instead of fear.*

- Breathe in: *Inner Guide, I welcome your voice of love to be my internal teacher.*

- Breathe out: *With love as my guide, I expect miracles.*

- Now sit in stillness and let the voice of love come forward.

Day 7

REFLECT AND PREPARE

We close out each week by reflecting on the past week and reading the introduction to the upcoming week. So today, spend some cozy time in your meditation space and take a moment to reflect on your work this week. You may want to highlight certain passages or exercises in your journal that were powerful for you. You might even want to repeat one of your meditations or journaling exercises.

I'll layer each week's work into the next, so don't hesitate to bring your tools with you as we continue on this journey.

When you're finished with your reflecting, it's time to read the introduction to Week Two. Week Two's introduction will deepen your practice of self-love and strengthen your faith in love. Get ready to throw down some self-love and expect miracles!

WEEK 2

A NEW
SELF-PERCEPTION

*The most common way
people give up their power
is by thinking they
don't have any.*

—Alice Walker

S ometimes the phrase "self-love" gets a bad rap. Many folks balk at the concept because they may perceive it as too New Age or narcissistic. But for the sake of your happiness, let's forget about semantics and open up to the idea of self-love. It's the key ingredient for internal power and it's essential to your miracle mind-set.

I describe self-love as the place we come to when we let go of everything else. In a recent interview, I was asked, "Do you love who you've become?" My response was, "I don't believe I've become anyone, I've just released all that was blocking me from who I really am." When we release our ego's false perception of who we are or who we need to be, we can surrender to the truth, which is that we *are* love. The love that I speak of is an intuitive voice reminding us we're great and worthy, leading us in the right direction and helping us let go of resentment and return to peace. This inner presence has been stifled, but through the practice of self-forgiveness and acceptance we can reawaken this peaceful self-love state. By following the guided suggestions this week, you'll see your self-hatred and doubt begin to release. You will awaken a new relationship with your inner state of love—the most important relationship in your life.

When you reestablish a loving relationship with yourself,

you begin to realize how self-love is no different from the love you show others. A *Course in Miracles* teaches us that when we attack ourselves, we attack the world; and when we love ourselves, we love the world. A self-inflicted attack has a direct effect on the energy around you. Therefore, if you consistently attack yourself, you are consistently attacking the world. Sounds serious, right? It is. Self-attack leads to low-level energy. That energy spreads like a virus. The more people who function from a place of fear and low-level energy, the more violence, war, and hate there is. If we want to have a positive impact, we must become spiritual activists committed to changing the world one loving thought at a time.

A lack of self-love can lead you down many dark paths. You can feel incomplete and therefore feel the need to "complete" others so you can feel worthy and "good enough." Lack of self-love can also have the opposite effect: you can feel so angry with yourself that you isolate and deny the world your beautiful gifts.

For instance, in the case of my dear friend Christine Arylo, her lack of self-love led her to a deep bottom that later became the catalyst for her greatest change. Christine was a self-proclaimed achievement junkie, and she suffered from codependency. Her need for outside approval from everyone she met reflected her inner disapproval. Christine couldn't love herself, so she needed the world to compensate for what was missing. On the outside, she seemed to have it all: the fiancé, the six-figure corporate job, the comfortable home, and all the necessary trappings of a "happy person"—but on the inside she was a mess. Striving for outside approval and love led Christine to inner turmoil and a constant state of feeling overwhelmed.

When you search for your self-worth in external circumstances, you will never feel fulfilled. You'll be on an endless search, struggling to find "enough" approval and love. Christine was searching for love in all the wrong places.

Then one day in 2001, Christine got a wake-up call that would change her life. As she drove to her engagement party, her fiancé called her to announce that he didn't love her or want to marry her anymore, and he was calling off the wedding. As you can imagine, this proclamation rocked Christine to her core. Her immediate response was to isolate and go into a serious state of self-hatred, berating herself with negative thoughts like, *This is your fault* or *You'll never have a healthy relationship.* To make matters worse, her ego took over and placed blame on her fiancé. The *Course* teaches us that one of the ego's greatest tricks is to project our fear onto others to avoid having to deal with the discomfort. This false defense mechanism only hurts us more.

Once the initial shock wore off, Christine had two choices. She could turn the situation into another reason to hate herself, or she could see it as her opportunity to change. She chose change. Christine surrendered to the pain of rejection and allowed herself to be broken open. Instead of choosing to stay resentful forever, she chose to let go and invite miracles to occur. We all face this decision at some point in our lives. Oftentimes, hitting bottom gives us the opportunity to recognize that there has to be a better way. Hitting bottom was the greatest gift she received. Her bottom became a turning point and a time for her to take all the necessary steps to turn inward and establish her own practice of love. And she did just that. One day at a time Christine rebuilt her inner state of self-love through affirmations, prayer, self-kindness, meditation, and a serious for-giveness practice. In short, she took focused and positive action. She reignited her relationship to herself. Upon reconnecting to this state of peace Christine went through a steadfast spiritual process to forgive her fiancé and choose to perceive him as a gift. The gift of self-love was given to her.

Today Christine is known as the Queen of Self-Love. She is the author of the book *Madly in Love with Me* and lectures throughout the country on the topic of self-love, and she has made it her mission to guide others to know their greatness. Christine turned her problem into her purpose, and today is a powerful example for the world.

I hope Christine's story empowers you to dive deep into this week's exercises. Maybe you've been struggling with codepen-dency or self-hatred. Maybe your self-attack is at an all-time high. Or maybe it's subtler, and your lack of self-love comes out through your relationship to food, drugs, or sex. Regardless of how you may be acting out, know that each of us has discon-nected in some way from our relationship to love within. And each of us has the power to reignite that connection.

Much like Christine, we all need to reconnect with our sense of self-love if we're going to live with miracle minds. So once again, open your heart, mind, and notebook and prepare for another week of transformational shifts.

Though this week is focused on self-love, it's important to understand that *A Course in Miracles* does not emphasize the "self." The *Course* perceives all self-perception as separation from our truthful state of oneness. When we place too much emphasis on our self (good or bad), the ego is convincing us we're special, either more special than others or less special. The goal is to let go of our ego's self-perception over time and eventually remember that we are equal to others.

The ego works hard to keep us stuck in self-attack—even when it seems like we're attacking others. When we're hooked into the ego's perception of self, we often compare ourselves to others. Comparing leads to self-inflicted judgment and attack. The ego needs to compare us to others to reinforce the illusion that we are less than or better than others. For instance, you may compare yourself to a coworker who makes more money than you. The ego response is to attack your coworker and judge her for having what you want. In effect, the ego has convinced you that because your coworker has what you want, *you'll never have it*. This is the ego mentality that there isn't enough to go around. This ego's comparing reinforces your judgment toward others and the lack you perceive in yourself. The *Course* reminds us throughout the text that when we judge others, we're judging ourselves. Comparing and judgment are the catalysts for much internal chaos and dark inner turmoil. Don't get hung up about this: the exercises this week will guide you to use your ego's self-perception as a learning device for true growth.

Your practice this week will enable you to bring your wrong-minded ego perceptions of yourself to your ~ing for healing. Shining love on the way you perceive your "self" will help you to see that your misplaced thoughts are just illusions, and it will help you restore the faith that you *are* love. In the subtle moments when you recognize this truth, a miracle occurs. In an instant, you can remember that you're equal to everyone and that we are all love. The more you practice these principles, the more you will release the negative "self" your ego created and reconnect to the love that you are.

Here's the plan:

- On **Day 8**, you're going to bust out your magnifying glass and begin the witnessing process. You'll be led to consciously assess the ways you've been attacking, doubting, and abusing yourself. Looking closely at this behavior may feel uncomfortable at first, but know that you're in a safe container to hold these feelings. Know you're being guided.
- On **Day 9**, we'll throw down some willingness— remember that willingness is crucial for creating change.
- On **Day 10**, you'll ignite some new perceptions. I'll lead you to turn your fears upside down and change your mind about your relationship to yourself.
- **Day 11** brings us back to gratitude, and you'll focus on what you love about yourself and your life.
- On **Day 12** we start dropping some F bombs and going big with serious self-Forgiveness.
- **Day 13** we welcome in the miracles . . .
- . . . and on **Day 14** we review and prepare for the forthcoming week.

You're starting to see the pattern, right? Soon this practice will become second nature. That's how it can be a lifelong way.

Before you jump into your self-love practice, make sure to be extra kind to yourself this week. Prepare tonight by cleaning your room, maybe map out some healthy meals, and make sure to drink lots of water. Stay hydrated, healthy, and well rested throughout the week. We're going deep this week, and we'll be dredging up some old stuff that's been hiding out for decades. Your self-care will greatly support you as you open up to deal with and heal old wounds.

Day 8

WITNESS YOUR
SELF-INFLICTED FEAR

Are you aware of how unkind you can be toward yourself? Sometimes we don't even realize how nasty we have been. Do you ever tell yourself that you're not good enough, smart enough, thin enough, and so on? Do you play small by shying away from what you desire? Are you abusing your body with substances, food, sex, and so on? Are you unwilling to forgive yourself for something in the past?

It's likely that whether you realize it or not, in one or more of these ways you've been unkind to yourself. It's okay, my friend. How could you have known otherwise? Remember that as a young child you picked up all kinds of limiting beliefs and patterns. These thought patterns have been replaying in your day-to-day life and have established the type of relationship you have with yourself today. But now all that will change. This week's work will create a new self-love blueprint that will realign you with a loving relationship to self. Let's begin with your morning reflection.

■ Morning Reflection **DAY 8**

This morning's reflection requires that you fearlessly witness how your thoughts have created your reality. I know it's tough to take responsibility for your experiences, but your practice will help you accept the true power you have to create a new, more loving reality. Sit in your meditation space and take a deep breath. When you're ready, read the morning passage that follows. Then sit for one minute of stillness and let the words settle in.

A COURSE IN MIRACLES PRAYER

I am responsible for what I see.
I choose the feelings I experience and
I decide upon the good I would achieve.
And, everything that happens to me
I ask for, and receive as I have asked.

Affirmation Day 8

ଅ I AM RESPONSIBLE FOR WHAT I SEE.

Today's affirmation sustains your witnessing process. Repeat this affirmation throughout the day and remember the power you have to choose your perspective.

As you use your affirmation throughout the day you'll become more aware of how you've chosen to perceive the world around you. Let go and know this opening is the first step to healing your connection to self. True self-love requires radical self-reflection. *A*

Course in Miracles emphasizes the importance of shining light on the ego's darkness. Taking responsibility for your ego's fear is a major step toward letting yourself off the hook. Once you can see that you simply made a wrong-minded choice, you can consciously choose the right mind instead. Try not to get upset with yourself when you look at the ego's delusions. Instead be proud that you're looking upon your fears with the intention of transforming them.

■ Evening Exercise **DAY 8**

Now that you're home for the day, let's go deeper into self-reflection. Head over to your meditation space and answer the following questions in your journal. Take your time with this exercise— there is no need to rush it. Get honest with each answer. This is an exercise in *~ing* writing. An *~ing* write is a stream-of-consciousness writing exercise in which you let your pen flow and allow the words to glide onto the page. Don't edit anything. Let your subconscious mind write through you to uncover your truth. Answer the following questions with an *~ing* write and let it all come out.

- How have I been unkind to myself?
  ~ing-write your response . . .
- How have I been playing small?
  ~ing-write your response . . .
- What is the negative story I have created about myself?
  ~ing-write your response . . .

- How have I abused myself with my thoughts or actions?

~ing-write your response . . .

When you're finished, take a moment to reflect on what you've written. Remember not to judge yourself for anything you put on the page. A *Course in Miracles* emphasizes the principle of nonjudgment. Fear wants to judge, whereas love wants to forgive. So be kind to yourself when reflecting on this work. Be the gentle witness.

Uncomfortable feelings may come up. Take this as a good sign. Allow yourself to experience all the thoughts and feelings that come over you throughout this practice. Feeling is healing, so get comfortable being uncomfortable and trust that love is guiding your path.

Day 9

BECOME WILLING TO LOVE YOURSELF

The way we treat ourselves all comes down to one decision: the decision of love. Deciding for love is a commitment that requires willingness. When we're unwilling to deal with our past or unwilling to look at our patterns, true change cannot occur. Living with a miracle mind is a deep process. It requires a true surrender to look at your fears head-on and say, "I am willing to change." By picking up this book, you've already made a statement to the Universe. You announced your willingness to shift and grow.

Now let's take it one step further. Become willing to love yourself fully. It may seem tough to awaken the willingness to love yourself. This is to be expected. The ego has worked very hard to convince us we're unlovable. Mustering up the desire to love oneself may seem like a hefty feat. Try not to get tripped up about this. Instead, keep it simple and allow today's morning reflection to guide your process. Follow the exercises and allow willingness to shine forth.

Having the willingness is all you need to receive the

guidance to change. With that in mind, today's practice is less action based and more subconscious. This work is about surrender.

■ Morning Reflection DAY 9

Begin today's morning reflection in your meditation space. Sit on the floor or even get on your knees to read the passage. The gesture of getting on your knees is a reflection of true surrender. When I surrendered to release my negative self-perceptions, I spent several months praying on my knees. This physical act of praying on my knees made a statement to myself, and the energy around me that I was ready, willing, and able to love myself again. So if you're up for it, hit your knees and read the following passage out loud. Then sit for one minute of stillness and let the love settle in.

> *I surrender. Today I turn over all the fearful projections that I have placed upon myself. I release all self-doubt and attack today. In this moment, I choose to let it all go. I am willing to be guided to new projections. I am willing to love myself again. Inner Guide, please take the steering wheel and show me how to truly surrender my fear so I can wholeheartedly love myself again.*

Affirmation Day 9

**I AM WILLING TO LET GO OF MY SELF-DOUBT.
I SURRENDER TO SELF-LOVE.**

When you sense fear sneak in today, it's important that you consciously reach for your affirmation. As you become more aware of the ways in which you treat yourself poorly, you heighten your willingness to choose love. Here are some things to look out for: negative self-talk, attack thoughts toward yourself, comparing yourself to others, or judging yourself wrongly. Genuine awareness is key to transcending all wrong-minded decisions. Today be diligent as you work with your affirmation. You may even want to write it on a piece of paper or a bright Post-it and tape it to your computer screen or somewhere that you look throughout the day. The visual reminder of your affirmation is a subtle but powerful way to imprint it on your consciousness.

■ Evening Exercise **DAY 9**

This evening's check-in is all about self-care. As I mentioned in the introduction to this week, it's essential that you take care of yourself throughout this process. Your willingness to look at your self-attack is very powerful, but it can also bring up uncomfortable feelings. Today's surrender may have cracked you open even more. Therefore, this evening, do something kind for yourself. For instance, make yourself a cup of tea and sit peacefully in your meditation space for ten minutes. Or light a candle, cook a meal for yourself, or take a long bath or shower. Whatever you choose to do, treat yourself like an innocent child. Nurture yourself in some way.

Then before you go to sleep tonight, close your day with an evening reflection that will deepen your willingness. Like you did for the morning exercise, I suggest you get on your knees once again and pray. Remember that this work is totally non-denominational. The practice of praying on your knees just represents surrender. If this makes you feel uncomfortable in any way, then simply sit on a pillow and say your prayer out loud.

Inner Guide, thank you for your work today. Tonight I deepen my commitment to self-love and ask that you remove from me all self-doubt, all attack thoughts, and all my limiting beliefs. I surrender my relationship to myself to you. Inner Guide, thank you for mending this relationship and reigniting love.

Day 10

I CHOOSE TO LOVE MYSELF TODAY

Today's work reminds you once again that choosing love over fear truly is your choice. Throughout the day I'll lead you to renounce your self-attack and choose a more loving perspective. Today begins the pattern of a whole new way of communicating with yourself. Establishing a new self-dialogue is a crucial step toward becoming more self-loving. What you say to yourself *unconsciously* becomes what you *consciously* believe about yourself. Today, let's clean up the conversation. Let's begin with your morning reflection.

■ Morning Reflection **DAY 10**

Get cozy in your meditation space. Sit up straight and take a deep breath in through your nose and exhale it out your mouth. Read the following passage out loud to yourself, then sit quietly for a minute to absorb the words.

*I am love. Everything in me and outside of me is love. Today
I choose to repeat this, believe this, and commit to this. I am
love. Anything else I have chosen to believe is false evidence
appearing real. What I choose to see as real today is love and
only love. I am love.*

Affirmation Day 10

I AM LOVE.

Today's affirmation is simple. Throughout the day, when you
notice self-attack or self-judgment, say gently to yourself: *I am
love.* The simple gesture of reminding yourself that you *are* love
will be your guide.

■ Evening Exercise DAY 10

This evening's exercise is based on inspirational teacher Louise
Hay's most powerful tool. Make sure to have a box of tissues
nearby . . . this is some majorly transformational work!

This exercise requires a mirror. Grab a hand mirror or a
makeup compact. Bring the mirror into your meditation space.
Look at yourself directly in the mirror and say, "I love you." Say
this out loud at least three times as you stare at yourself directly
in the mirror. Let go, release, and don't edit your emotions. Just
let love take over.

This exercise may bring up several emotions—maybe even
some you feel totally unprepared for. The first time I did this
exercise I felt awkward and uncomfortable. Affirming self-love

in the mirror was the opposite of what I'd been taught to do, and it made me feel almost embarrassed.

All kinds of difficult emotions can come up when you practice this exercise. Therefore, I've added a bedtime practice of simple self-reflective journaling. After you've affirmed self-love in the mirror, ~*ing*-write for ten minutes or more. Let your pen flow and allow your emotions to come forward. The topic of this ~*ing* write is: *I choose to love myself fully.* Let the writing begin . . .

Day 11

SELF-GRATITUDE

Today we bring back the attitude of gratitude. This practice will awaken your loving mind throughout the day and remind you of your greatness that, until now, has likely been hidden and ignored. Keep it simple. Your ego's probably done a great job of convincing you that there's nothing (or very little) to be grateful for. Try to dig even deeper, and reach into your love center to focus on what you appreciate about yourself. Let's get the ball rolling with this morning's reflection.

■ Morning Reflection **DAY 11**

Sit comfortably in your meditation space and read the morning reflection. Be mindful not to judge this process. Your ego will resist this work and may convince you that there's little to be grateful for. Try your best to listen to love today. As you read the passage, connect to the simplicity of what gratitude has to offer you. After reading, sit in stillness for one minute to let this radical idea of self-gratitude soak into your cells.

> *Today I am grateful for who I am. I am grateful for the air I breathe, for the food I eat, for the place I lay my head at night. I am grateful for the lessons I have learned and for the process I am in. I am grateful for my willingness to change my mind and choose love over fear. My gratitude for myself fills me with joy and unleashes my miracle mind.*

Affirmation Day 11

I AM GRATEFUL FOR THIS MOMENT.

Today's affirmation can be used throughout the day. In simple experiences like catching the train or enjoying a cup of tea, simply say the affirmation. Even when things seem to be going wrong, say to yourself, *I am grateful for this moment.* Let this affirmation lead you out of ego fear and into gratitude. The attitude of gratitude is like water for the miracle-minded person. The more you drink, the clearer you feel. Enjoy this refreshing affirmation.

■ Evening Exercise DAY 11

When you're settled back in from the day, take a moment to center into your meditation space. Grab your notebook and sit comfortably on the floor. Take a few deep breaths in your nose and exhale them through your mouth. As you breathe, allow yourself the gift of letting go of the day. Just breathe in and experience your emotions—and on the exhale, release them. Take ten deep breaths in and release.

This simple breathing exercise will help you center into your love energy. Now that you've got your ~ing on, let's call on love to come forward and reinforce your gratitude. In your notebook, write a gratitude list. This list is specifically focused on what you're grateful for about yourself. The list might include gratitude for everything from your bed to your ability to care for others or your open mind. Try not to get tripped up about this. No matter how dark your ego's self-projections have been, you can always reach for hope. When I was newly sober and beginning my spiritual practice, I focused on being grateful for every detail of my life. I was grateful for waking up without a hangover, I was grateful that I remembered what I'd done the night before, I was even grateful that I had the energy to brush my teeth. Being grateful for the simple stuff encouraged me to move forward with my recovery and helped me celebrate everything in my life. Dig deep into your love bank and grab some gratitude for yourself. Make your list and sit with it for a moment. Reread it a few times and let it sink in. Then do the exercise with the following self-gratitude meditation.

You can follow my guidance here or visit www.gabbyb.tv/meditate for the guided audio meditations.

SELF-GRATITUDE MEDITATION

- Get comfortable in your bed or your meditation space.

- Sit up straight and pull your shoulders back.

- Prepare your body to be a vessel to receive loving energy.

- Take a deep breath in through your nose, exhaling it out your mouth.

- Continue this cycle of breath throughout your meditation.

- Breathe in though your nose.

- Breathe out through your mouth.

- As you continue this cycle of breath, recite your self-gratitude list in your mind.

- One by one go down the list and call on the love you cultivated today.

- Breathe in the gratitude.

- Exhale and extend your gratitude.

- Allow this list to take energetic form in your body.

- Loving thoughts will guide you to loving energy.

- Breathe in: *I am grateful for* _____.

- Breathe out: *I am grateful for* _____.

- Breathe in: *I am grateful for* _____.

- Breathe out: *I am grateful for* _____.

- Breathe in: *I am grateful for* _____.

- Breathe out: *I am grateful for* _____.

- Let love flow.

- Continue breathing your gratitude list in and out.

- When you're ready, open your eyes to the room.

Day 12

THE F WORD

Not that F word, but forgiveness.

Forgiveness is like air: we need it to survive. The miracle mind-set requires a serious commitment to forgiveness, and the process begins by first forgiving yourself. Carrying a past resentment toward yourself is what has kept you stuck in old fear patterns and has held you back from living a free-flowing life of love. Maybe you cannot move forward in your career because you can't forgive yourself for making mistakes in the past. Or maybe you cannot forgive yourself for hurting someone in the past and now you're afraid of intimacy altogether. The guilt you carry around keeps you stuck in the past and afraid of the future. A *Course in Miracles* says, ". . . holding no prisoner to guilt, we become free." Today's practice will be the first step toward setting yourself free from the bondage of self-attack and guilt.

You may have no idea how to begin the self-forgiveness process. Try not to get hung up about the *how* and instead *allow.*

Trust that your inner guide has your back and is leading you on this path. When you accept forgiveness as your plan for happiness, then love will lead the way. Surrender to today's exercises and allow miracles to occur naturally. Let's throw down the F word with your morning reflection!

■ Morning Reflection **DAY 12**

Today we begin with a morning reflection that will ignite your self-forgiveness practice. Sit comfortably in your meditation space. Breathe deeply in through your nose and exhale out through your mouth. When you're ready, read the passage. Then sit for one minute of stillness and marinate in the message.

> *For today I commit to letting go of my past. In this moment I choose to release all the pent-up anger and resentment I have placed on myself. I welcome even a moment of release. I forgive myself for my past, my present, and my future. I trust that I am love and that all my life's experiences have been divinely placed for me to learn and grow. I've done the best I can with my life's circumstances, and today the best I can do is forgive. I forgive myself today.*

Affirmation Day 12

⚘ I FORGIVE MYSELF FOR HAVING THIS THOUGHT.
⚘ I CHOOSE LOVE INSTEAD.

Today's affirmation is a forgiveness affirmation that I suggest you use for the rest of your life. I say it all throughout the day, every day. Whenever a fearful thought comes through my mind, I replace it with my F word affirmation. Throughout the day, when you notice yourself fill up with fear or self-resentment, simply say, "I forgive myself for having this thought. I choose love instead." Forgiving the ego for having a particular negative thought is a very powerful tool. In the moment that you forgive the thought, you're acknowledging that *you are not your fear.* You can see the fear for what it really is: an ego projection you've chosen to believe in, not who you truly are. Each time you offer yourself this affirmation, you strengthen your self-love.

In some cases you may not even realize that fear has you in a headlock. For instance, many people walk around all day judging and attacking themselves and others with small but powerful negative thoughts. This is the ego's fear taking over. Or you may be thinking negatively toward someone who has hurt you. The ego has convinced you to believe that this hurt warrants attack, but in truth, the negative thoughts are only harming you more. Become mindful of the ways you attack, judge, separate, and replay negativity in your mind. Then, throughout the day, respond to your fear-driven thoughts with the affirmation, *I forgive myself for having this thought. I choose love instead.*

■ Evening Exercise **DAY 12**

Now that you're settling back in from your day, take time to reflect on the power of your affirmation. Answering the following questions will help you internalize the work. It can be powerful to reflect on your inner journey so that you can witness your growth. Remember that the true change occurs in the subtle shifts—therefore, highlight and honor even the simplest change.

Answer the following questions in your journal:

1. How did it feel to see your fearful thoughts as separate from you?
2. What kind of relief did you experience from practicing your affirmation?
3. Did your affirmation stop you from acting out with self-destructive behavior?
4. Are you committed to practicing this self-forgiveness affirmation all the time?

Looking closely at today's practice helps you center into the progression of the work. It is important to reflect on your journey. The shifts occur naturally, and shining light on them allows you to celebrate your change. Remember always to look at your practice from a loving perspective. The ego will want to sabotage your hard work and find fault in everything. Be mindful of this and remain the nonjudgmental witness of your powerful transformation.

To complete this exercise, let's close the day with a prayer. Sit comfortably in your meditation space and recite the following prayer out loud:

Divine guidance that surrounds me, I welcome your support. I recognize where my mind has gone wrong and I can see how unforgiving I have been. I see my part in creating this pattern of self-destruction and I welcome spirit to step in. I am willing to see love instead of this. Thank you for your guidance in my self-forgiveness practice. I will listen to my intuition, show up for my spiritual assignments, and do all that is necessary to love myself again. Show me what you got . . .

Day 13

GO BIG AND
EXPECT MIRACLES

Today's practice is powerful. The simple shifts throughout the past week and a half have begun to invite miracles. Now it's time to begin anticipating miraculous shifts. The more you expect miracles, the more miracles you will experience. Miracles are available to us all. We just need to be faithful to and aware of their presence.

So today let's work on accepting your inner peace and self-love fully, which will heighten your miracle mind-set. Each passage, affirmation, and exercise will lead you to deepen this belief system. This work is superimportant early in your practice. A full commitment is required to take the next right actions. So for today, let's catapult your miracle mind-set and rock out with your inner faith!

■ **Morning Reflection DAY 13**

Get centered in your meditation space. Write down in your journal, *Today I commit to miraculous shifts. Forgiveness will be my guide.* Then take a deep breath in through your nose and breathe out through your mouth. When you're ready, read your morning passage out loud to yourself. Afterward, sit in stillness for one minute and soak up the day's first miracle.

> *Each moment I choose to forgive my fear, I see love instead. This is a miracle. For today I will add up these miraculous shifts and enjoy the loving support I receive from the Universe. Love and miracles are available to me now. Through the practice of self-love and forgiveness a miracle is bestowed upon me.*

Affirmation Day 13

TODAY I COMMIT TO MIRACULOUS SHIFTS. FORGIVENESS WILL BE MY GUIDE.

Your affirmation today reinforces the words in your morning reflection passage. Whenever you notice your ego act out, say your affirmation. Use it when you notice your self-judgment rise up. Rather than go deeper into self-attack, simply drop your affirmation into the mix and let love take over. Enjoy the moment-to-moment miracles and let them add up.

■ Evening Exercise **DAY 13**

As you settle in from your day, take a five-minute self-reflection break. Go into your meditation space and read the following prayer. This exercise is awesome because it allows you to release the forgiveness process to the care of your inner guide. The F word can be tough to comprehend at times—especially when it comes to self-forgiveness. So for today, simply turn your desire to forgive over to spirit and let your ~ing do her thing.

SELF-FORGIVENESS PRAYER

Inner Guide, I welcome your support. I have made the commitment to forgive myself and I am ready to release the chains that fear has placed upon me. I know forgiveness will set me free. I turn this desire over to you and I accept that you will show me where to go, what to do, and what to say. I know you will lead me to the perfect assignments and lessons so that I can deepen my self-love and release my fear. Thank you for guiding me to forgive myself.

To close the day, let's rock out with an F word meditation that is geared toward forgiving yourself. Prepare to do some ~ing writing immediately following the meditation. This process is likely to make you want to unload in your journal and let go of some old self-resentments. Stay open to the process and allow my meditation to guide you. You can read the meditation here or download the audio meditation from www.gabbyb.tv/meditate.

SELF-FORGIVENESS MEDITATION

- Sit comfortably in your meditation space.

- Gently pull your shoulders back and keep your palms facing upward.

- Take a deep breath in through your nose and exhale out your mouth.

- Continue this cycle of breath throughout the meditation.

- As you continue this cycle of breath, begin to envision yourself as an innocent child.

- Allow your mind's eye to bring forth your childhood image.

- Try not to interfere with this image.

- Allow your subconscious mind to guide you to see your innocent child self.

- As you continue breathing in your nose and out your mouth, let your mind wander.

- Hold the image of your innocent child playing, laughing, and enjoying life.

- Do your best to reconnect to this time.

- As you deepen this vision of your child self, begin to breathe in and out the following affirmations.

- Breathe in: *I am innocent.*

- Breathe out: *I am love.*

- Breathe in: *I am not wrong.*

- Breathe out: *I have not sinned.*

- Breathe in: *I am guiltless.*

- Breathe out: *I am whole.*

- Breathe in: *I am good enough.*

- Breathe out: *I am love.*

- Continue these mantras for as long as you wish.

When you're ready, pick up your notebook and begin ~*ing* writing. Let your subconscious thoughts flow onto the page. Don't edit a word—just let them flow. When you're finished with your ~*ing* write, cozy up in bed or spend some quiet time alone. If you don't live alone, you can be mindful to create quiet space. When I first moved in with my fiancé, I had to find ways to create private space for my practice. Sometimes I'd meditate in the bath to get the sacred time alone. Do what you can to create this space and trust that your shift in energy will greatly benefit everyone in your home (even your pets). Let this powerful work set in. Don't turn on the TV or engage in any deep conversations. Trust that this process is deep and is opening you up to spiritual shifts. Be still.

Day 14

REFLECT AND PREPARE

Today let's look back at the incredible work you've done so far.

■ Morning Reflection DAY 14

For this morning's reflection, take a moment to look through your notebook and witness the learning and healing that has come forward. You may find that the work you're doing can be a bit uncomfortable. Or maybe you feel a little stuck in one of the exercises. That's totally fine. A *Course in Miracles* suggests, "Only infinite patience offers immediate results." As you continue your practice, make patience your greatest virtue. Each still moment of patience offers you the space to receive divine guidance from your ~*ing*. Be kind and gentle with yourself and throughout the rest of this forty-two-day practice, making patience a top priority.

As you review this past week be very mindful not to look for problems in your work. *A Course in Miracles* asks, "Do you want the problem or do you want the answer?" Stay committed to seeking the answer and trust that as you open up to receive guidance you will always be led to the next right action. Creating sacred space to review your work without judgment will help you on your journey of acknowledging the answer, which is that *you are love*.

■ Evening Exercise **DAY 14**

Your next and final exercise for this week is to prepare for next week's work. In the coming week we will delve into your relationship to your body. Fear shows up in some supernasty ways when it comes to our body image and physical health. I hope this chapter gives you a new, incredible perspective and heightens your awareness of the possibility for miracles. Change your mind about your body, and your body will change. Enjoy Week Three's introduction and get ready to take your miraculous practice to a whole new level!

WEEK 3

BODY IMAGE

*Our bodies are a vehicle for
spiritual growth and healing.*

I believe that we are spirits having a human experience. What do I mean by this? Now, this is a loaded statement—so let me break it down for you Spirit Junkie style. Through my *Course* work I've come to understand that the body is a learning device for us to reconnect to our true essence, which is love. In our bodies, we can go through a lot of funky assignments to ultimately return to our spiritual faith in love. A *Course in Miracles* teaches us to use our body to show up for these assignments and learn spiritual lessons. This process can be difficult at times, but it allows us to recognize that we are here in our body to transcend our fear of the world and communicate the lessons of love.

The ego cannot comprehend the concept of the body as a learning device. The ego has convinced us that our body is who we are. We've identified with our ego perception of being fat, tall, short, black, white, crippled, sick, and so on. The ego compares the body to other bodies. The ego wants us to use the body to get more from the world—whether it's sex, money, or success. Worst of all, the ego convinces us to be afraid of the body.

I can safely say that most of us, at some point in time, have had a negative relationship to our body. Experiencing our body through our ego's eyes will always kick up feelings of inadequacy and separateness. When we succumb to the thoughts of our ego, we experience low-level thoughts, which negatively affect our body's energy field. If we're constantly attacking ourselves with nasty thoughts, the energy behind those thoughts seeps into our body—and that low-level energy is powerful, whether we realize it or not. In its worst form, this negative energy can manifest as illness, which in turn reinforces fear. When we carry around resentments, self-hatred, and judgment, we attack our bodies with low-level thoughts and energy. The fear we carry is like a virus in our minds, and eventually that virus can take over our bodies. As we begin to understand how our energy affects our bodies, we will come to see how spiritual healing will greatly support physical healing.

From the *Course*'s perspective, each time we perceive our body with judgment or attack by comparing it to other bodies, we are separating ourselves from our truthful state: love. And each time we separate from love, we feel (to put it bluntly) like crap. We think we feel bad because our body isn't good enough or because the world told us we were fat, ugly, poor, and so on. But the real reason we feel so terrible is because we are separated from love. This disassociation from love makes us feel an unconscious guilt. We experience this guilt because deep down we know that ultimately we're responsible for disconnecting from our loving truth. *A Course in Miracles* describes this guilt as though we've disassociated with love, a.k.a. God, and in essence we've killed our connection to love. This ignites the ego's unconscious guilt. Even though the guilt exists below our level of consciousness, we feel its pain and want to numb it. The ego works hard to anesthetize this feeling of guilt by hooking us into fearful patterns, from overeating and body dysmorphia to substance abuse, unhealthy sexual behavior, and so on. Why? These behaviors strengthen the ego's spiral and keep us locked into fear. Think about your own behavior. When you feel uncomfortable, it's likely you turn to fearful thoughts, actions, and behavior to avoid dealing with that discomfort. This is the ego's nasty trick of denial. When we deny our feelings of guilt, we go deeper into the fear and heighten our faith in the ego.

Fear is a hungry bottomless pit. For the ego to stay alive, fear must be fed. This is where our abuse of the body becomes unconscious and addictive. Whether we're abusing our body through our thoughts, actions, or beliefs, we're reinforcing fear one moment at a time to keep the ego satisfied and full.

For the first twenty-five years of my life, I was caught up in this type of ego perception of my body. I used my body to gain status. I thought that if I dressed my body in a short enough skirt, I could get the attention I sought so desperately. I spent years thinking my body was better than those a size bigger and hating my body for not being a size smaller. I abused it with drugs, food, alcohol, and stress. Worst of all, I abused my body with my thoughts. My ego ran the show—and as a result, I spent decades using the outside world to fortify my feelings of incompleteness.

The ego pattern and fearful projections I placed on my body made me physically ill in many ways. For instance, no matter how many times I tried to stop taking drugs, I couldn't let go of the addiction because I used the drugs to numb my unhealed pain. No matter how many times I tried to stop binge eating, I couldn't quit for fear of not having enough. Each of these abusive patterns was the result of a spiritual condition: I had separated from love and chose my ego's perception. All my body's disease was what many metaphysicians refer to as "dis-ease." My fearful body image created dis-ease in my mind and therefore affected my physical condition. Not to mention the harshest consequence: I was stuck in the ego's body fear spiral of needing to constantly find an outward solution for an inward condition. Overeating, overdrinking, and overly obsessing about my weight were among several of the ways this ego behavior manifested in my life.

By the time I hit my bottom at the age of twenty-five, my body had hit bottom, too. I was in my midtwenties and weighed ninety-nine pounds. I had six ulcers and a severe drug addiction. And all this physical illness was the result of a spiritual condition.

Upon hitting bottom, I had no choice but to get sober and heal my fear-based perceptions. Through my spiritual practice, my body began to heal itself naturally. During my recovery I learned to have a loving perspective of my body. Then, as I grew to become a full-on Spirit Junkie, my body's real purpose became clear to me. I learned that my body (and all its functions) was the vehicle through which I would share an empowering message with the world. This realization gave me all the inspiration I've needed to stay healthy and fit for the work I am here to do. As a speaker, writer, and raconteur for love, I consciously use my body as a messenger for helping others awaken their spirits and start on their own spiritual paths.

Today, armed with this new understanding of my body's purpose, I am extremely conscious of how I treat my body. Because I understand that my body is here to be a messenger for transformation, I'm highly aware of how my thoughts and actions affect my physical condition. This level of awareness and spiritual commitment enables me to maintain a life of sobriety. I eat clean, healthy food and give my body the physical exercise it needs. Most important, I feed myself loving thoughts, reinforcing my miracle mind-set one moment at a time. Living in this way provides me the energy, health, and glow that I need to shine from the inside out and be an authentic guide.

The *Course* suggests that the body can serve one of two masters: the ego or your ~*ing*. When we have an ego perception of the body, it serves an ongoing purpose to prove specialness and separation, whereas when the body serves love, we allow our ~*ing* to lead us to right perception. Our inner guide looks at the ego as an illusion, seeing its lies and false projections. Upon realizing the loving purpose of the body, our inner guide uses the body as a learning device for deep growth and change. In my case, healing occurred when I stopped using my body to get something from the world and instead used it to serve the world. Bringing all physical illness to our inner guide for healing will lead us to know the true lessons behind what the body is trying to teach us. The body transforms from the ego's weapon into the ~*ing*'s vehicle for healing and extending love.

The Miracle

When you start to pay attention to how your thoughts affect your body, you become much more conscious of what you think. Whether you're an overeater, a heavy drinker, or a drug abuser, or you have a different issue, you'll come to know a new freedom.

When you change your mind about your body, your body changes. In fact, not only does your body change, but the purpose of the body shifts as well. Once you begin to see your body as love, you learn how to use it as a communication device for sharing that love.

Healing the Body the Miracle-Minded Way

The miracle-minded perspective on physical healing is much different from what we have been taught to believe in. The miracle mind-set does not aim to deny physical illness; it does, however, aim to establish a new way of perceiving the condition. The key principle to experiencing a miracle-minded perspective of the body is to welcome your ~*ing* in for healing. This practice requires that the mind be healed in order to support the healing of the body. Remember that fear in our mind creates illness in the body. Therefore, a mental cleanse is required to aid in the process of physical healing.

When you apply the thought system that your mind can aid in healing your body, you can experience many miracles. It's not that the physical condition just disappears (though it often does) but that you're guided to exactly who and what you need for healing to take place. When you welcome healing miracles, you'll see how spirit works through people to aid in your recovery. I've experienced miraculous physical healing as a result of turning over my life to my ~*ing*. For instance, I once had an experience where I caught a terrible flu while lecturing in Los Angeles. I was knocked out for several days. I had many meetings scheduled and I was hosting a huge lecture that weekend. Because I was in Los Angeles I was struggling to find a doctor who would take on new patients. I was bedridden and sicker than I'd been in years. Rather than succumb to the discomfort of the illness I prayed for guidance. I asked for a miracle. In my prayers I was willing to be guided to whatever it would take to get better. A few moments after my prayer I received a call from a friend. She suggested that I ask my doctor in New York for a referral. My uncreative ego mind hadn't thought of this when I was aggressively trying to get someone to help me in LA. I chose to follow my friend's suggestion and reach out to my doctor in New York by sending an S.O.S. e-mail to my doctor and dear friend, Dr. Frank Lipman. Frank responded in minutes, informing me that he had contacted a holistic doctor in Santa Monica who would see me that day based on his referral. Within the hour I was in the office of a man named Dr. De Mello. This doctor took me in with open arms and put me on intravenous vitamins. He shared my spiritual philosophies and holistic approach to health. Before putting the vitamin vial into the catheter he asked me to pray into the vitamins. The entire experience with Dr. De Mello was incredibly guided. I felt an invisible presence by our side working through him and through the vitamins. I was 99 percent better the next morning.

This is an example of what happens when you let love enter into the healing process. It's not that you just say a prayer and the illness is gone immediately (though that can happen). But the real miracle is that you allow the Universe to guide you to creative opportunities for healing. Maybe you're led to the right practitioner who will resonate with you and get to the root cause of your condition. Or possibly you're intuitively guided to a book that helps you heal your mind and body. I believe that spirit works through doctors and healers of all kinds to help guide your healing process. When you think with your ego, you block the guidance toward the right healing. When you think with love, you invite spirit to work through others to heal on your behalf.

Take this healing approach into your exercises this week, and I will guide you to address the root cause of all illness and destructive body behavior. When you bring these issues to the surface for healing, you will feel a sense of relief in simply knowing that there is a way out of your fear-based pattern. Pay attention to the guidance and trust that spirit is working on your behalf to heal your wrong-minded perceptions and guide you toward all that you need to heal your body.

The *Course* emphasizes that a miracle is a shift from body identification to spirit identification. When you surrender your thoughts to the care of your inner guide, spirit removes the limitations of the body and awakens your awareness of miracles. Throughout this week you will be guided to call on your *~ing* for a shift in perception from body identification to spirit identification, restoring your mind to the right perception of who you truly are. Check out all the great stuff you can expect in the week ahead:

- **Day 15** will be another witnessing exercise. This time you'll take a close look at the ways in which your ego has projected fear onto your body. Without judgment, you'll learn how your fear has created your body image.
- On **Day 16**, you'll be guided to surrender to the willingness to see your body in a new light. This

willingness will open you up to the rest of the week's exercises. In this practice, you'll invite the forgiving, loving presence of your ~ing to come forward and guide you instead of the ego's false perceptions. While choosing your ego as a guide just inflicts more pain and guilt, choosing your ~ing invites more joy and love. The miracle worker chooses ~ing—and experiences miraculous results.

- On **Day 17**, I'll guide you to choose a more loving perspective of your body. You will be led to flip your fears upside down and open up to a new perception of your physical being. You'll also be led to understand the true purpose of your body.

- **Day 18** is all about how gratitude is your attitude once again! You'll be led to focus on what you love about your body, thereby strengthening your right perceptions. Remember that the ego wants you to see your body as separate. But when you're grateful for your body's true purpose, which is to extend love, you dissociate from the specialness of your body and instead see it as one with everyone and everything. Gratitude awakens a new perception of your body.

- The work on **Day 19** is dedicated to forgiving yourself for the ways you've treated your body. The work you do on this day will be superhealing, and it will give you a sense of peace about your past thoughts and actions.

- On **Day 20**, you'll be guided to awaken your miracle mind-set of love. I'll lead you in exercises that will help you create a quantum shift in your body perception.

- On **Day 21**, I'll conclude the week's exercises with self-reflection and preparation. Then, in the evening, you'll prepare for the week to come by reading the introduction to the next chapter.

One day at a time we will break down your ego's body projections and awaken your faith in miracles. When you heal your thoughts about your body, true physical healing can occur. This week's work will teach you to use the body as a vehicle through which you learn transformational lessons and extend love to the world.

Day 15

A NEW REFLECTION

Today's work offers a new perception of your body far beyond what you may have been taught to believe. This day's work will help you understand how your ego has used your body as a weapon for keeping you stuck in the fear spiral of separation and specialness. Remember that the *Course* teaches that the ego teams up with the body to keep us stuck in fear. The ego compares our body to others, convincing us that our bodies are better or worse than others, strengthening the specialness and furthering our disassociation from oneness and a loving mind. To make matters worse, the ego uses the body to further separate us from love through mental and physical abuse and unhealthy lifestyle choices. It persuades us to believe that we're incomplete and lonely, then leads us to fill our body up with too much food, too much booze, too much sex—or deprive and starve our body as punishment.

The *Course* is emphatic that our choice for the ego is insane. Each of us in some way has chosen an insane belief about our body and therefore uses the body for the ego's benefit. It's likely that at some point in time you've been caught in an ego projection of your body. Without understanding the root cause of the issue, you felt powerless and stuck. Maybe you feel that way right now in this moment. Well, I've got fabulous news for you! I'm going to blow your ego out of the water today! I'm going to help you understand how your ego attacks the body, and I'll guide you to release the ego's projections by welcoming the true purpose of the body.

Let's begin today's practice with a witnessing exercise that will help you establish a greater understanding of how the ego has gotten you hooked into a negative body perception.

■ Morning Reflection DAY 15

Get comfortable in your meditation space and take a breath in through your nose and exhale out through your mouth. We are going deep today, and it's important that you call on your self-care work from last week to guide you through this process. Take a moment to read the following morning reflection and then sit for one minute of stillness to let the words settle in.

> *Today I will take a close look at how I've chosen the ego's fearful body image. I will get honest with myself about how I've been abusing my body with my thoughts, actions, food or substance intake, and more. I will not judge myself for the way I've treated my body; rather, I will love myself for looking at the ego and shining light on its darkness. Today I'm one step closer to freedom from body fear, and I am excited to begin this process.*

Affirmation Day 15

MY FALSE PERCEPTIONS OF MY BODY ARE
AN ATTACK. TODAY I CHOOSE LOVE INSTEAD OF
MY EGO'S PERCEPTIONS.

Today's affirmation is a simple reminder to witness your ego's body perception. This affirmation will also offer you a moment to check in with your body behavior throughout the day. So set your alarm on your phone for every hour on the hour. When the alarm goes off, reminding you of your Miracle Moment, repeat the affirmation.

Use your affirmation throughout the day when you catch your ego in the act. Recite this affirmation when you notice the following ego moments:

1. You compare your body to others.
2. You catch yourself overeating, starving, eating poorly, or engaging in any other negative food behavior.
3. You're using your body to reinforce your special projections of yourself. Some examples: you're using your body to get something from someone else, you're flaunting your body to feel better about yourself, or you're using your body to get positive reinforcement from others. In these moments, recite your affirmation and remind yourself: *My false perceptions of my body are an attack. Today I choose love instead of my ego's perceptions.*

Through this practice you'll begin the witnessing process, which blasts light onto the ego and highlights its falseness.

■ Evening Exercise DAY 15

After a full day of repeating your affirmation, you'll begin to recognize how your ego has used your body to reinforce more fear in your life. You may become more aware of your addictive patterns, or recognize for the first time how hard you are on yourself. Each time you call out your ego and take note of the chaotic thought, you get one step closer to disassociating from it. Witnessing your ego is one of the most valuable tools in this practice. This evening's tool will deepen your witnessing process through a writing exercise.

In your journal, take an inventory of all the ways your ego has used your body wrongly. Answer the following questions:

- What are my ego's fearful beliefs about my body?
- How are my negative thoughts affecting my energy?
- How has my ego made me think my body is special (better than others/separate)?
- How has my ego convinced me to see other bodies as more special?
- How have my fears from the past created negative body behaviors? (For instance, if your ego has held on to a past fear of feeling alone, then it's likely that you may fill your loneliness with food, sex, drugs, alcohol, etc.) In what ways have your ego body perceptions from the past negatively affected your behavior?

To close out the day, follow this bedtime exercise, which will help you recognize an important principle from the *Course*:

"Sickness is anger taken out upon the body so it will suffer pain." When you perceive your body negatively (physically ill, addicted, overweight, not good enough, etc.), you've chosen to take your ego's perception out on your body, thereby strengthening the ego. Tonight's work will help you recognize how the ego has used the body to reinforce more judgment, attack, separation, and guilt.

Take ten minutes before you sleep to ~ing-write in your journal. Write about all the ways your ego has convinced you that something is wrong with your body. Then write about how this ego perception has affected your body. This exercise lets your ~ing subconsciously guide you to witness how your ego has projected fear onto your body and, in doing so, convinced you that something is wrong.

The witnessing process is incredibly valuable for your spiritual growth. Why? Because when you recognize your ego's insanity, you wake up and remember how illusory your fear really is.

Day 16

MY BODY IS LIGHT

In today's practice, you'll invite the presence of your ~*ing* to come forward to help you heal your ego's false perception of your body. The *Course* says, "Perception is consistent with your choice, and . . . we choose between illusions and the truth, or pain and joy, or hell and heaven." This choice that the *Course* refers to is the decision to choose fear or love. Remember that by choosing the voice of the ego you're choosing to use your body as a weapon against love and as a tool for furthering your faith in separation. But when you choose to let your ~*ing* guide your thoughts, you'll be led to see love and use your body as a vehicle for extending more love. You become like an electrical transfer station. Energy comes into you and you convert it into even more energy, which then sheds light on the lives of hundreds, thousands, even millions of people. Today's work is to learn to rely on your ~*ing* to help you choose love over fear.

The basic goal for today's exercise is to once again invite your ~*ing* to heal your perceptions of your body. The *Course* states, "The body appears to be largely self-motivated and independent, yet it actually responds only to the intentions of the mind. . . . If the mind accepts the Holy Spirit's [~ing's] purpose for it instead . . . its kindly light shows all things from another point of view . . ."

So today you can stop trying to fix your body-image issues and fear, and instead welcome your ~ing to be your guide to new perceptions. Accept your ~ing as the inner voice that will lead you back to love.

■ Morning Reflection **DAY 16**

Sit comfortably in your meditation space and read the morning passage out loud. Then sit in stillness for one minute and let the passage set in.

> *Today I make an important decision. I decide to let my inner guide lead my thoughts about my body. I welcome the guidance of my ~ing to come forward and help me transform my ego's perceptions of my body. I welcome my ~ing to remind me of my body's true purpose, which is to be love and share love.*

Affirmation Day 16

I TURN MY PERCEPTION OF MY BODY OVER TO THE CARE OF MY INNER GUIDE. SHOW ME WHAT YOU'VE GOT . . .

Today's affirmation will be instrumental in guiding your perceptions. Set your alarm to go off three times throughout the day when you know you can take short breaks. In these

Miracle Moments, simply recite today's affirmation: *I turn my perception of my body over to the care of my inner guide. Show me what you've got . . .*

Don't overthink this affirmation. Simply take a moment when your alarm goes off, say your affirmation, and your internal surrender will occur naturally. This affirmation reiterates your willingness to choose love over fear—the simple choice that will begin to transform your false perceptions of your body.

■ Evening Exercise **DAY 16**

This evening's exercise begins with a prayer. Take a moment to sit in your meditation space and light a candle. In the stillness of this space, say the following prayer out loud:

> *Inner Guide, thank you for helping me release my false perceptions of my body. I recognize that I have chosen wrongly, and today I choose to forgive that choice. I choose your loving voice to replace my ego's fearful perceptions. I choose to let you guide me to use my body as a learning device for spiritual growth and service to the world.*

Following this prayer, spend some time listening to your inner guide. Through meditation I'll open you up to become conscious of your intuitive guidance and let your ~*ing* come through you. Engage in the following guided meditation or listen to the audio guide on www.gabbyb.tv/meditate. After your meditation, sit in stillness and listen. Let your ~*ing* step forward and lead you to a new body perception.

WILL~*ING* MEDITATION

- Find a comfortable seated position in your meditation space.

- Sit up straight with your palms facing upward.

- Take a deep breath in through your nose and breathe out through your mouth.

- Continue this cycle of breath throughout your meditation.

- Breathe in: *Inner Guide, I welcome your loving perspective to lead the way.*

- Breathe out: *I release my ego now.*

- Breathe in: *I am willing to perceive my body with love.*

- Breathe out: *I choose to release my fear.*

- Repeat these mantras with each inhale and exhale.

Allow yourself to settle into these words, and trust that you're awakening a connection to your inner guide.

Then sit in stillness and let the voice of spirit lead the way.

Day 17

WHAT DO I CHOOSE TO SEE IN THE MIRROR?

Today I'll guide you to choose a more loving perspective of your body. I've explained that the ego's false perceptions are not real, and once you fully commit to this concept, you're ready to return to love. Today's practice is based on Lesson 199 of *A Course in Miracles*: "I am not a body. I am free." The exercise of choosing your *~ing*'s perception of your body will help you let go of the form that the ego has placed upon it.

This work may be difficult for your ego to comprehend. As the *Course* says: "It is essential for your progress in this course that you accept today's idea, and hold it very dear. Be not concerned that to the ego it is quite insane. The ego holds the body dear because it dwells in it, and lives united with the home that it has made. It is a part of the illusion that has sheltered it from being found illusory itself." This passage reminds us that the ego will resist this work to keep us stuck in the illusion that the body is separate and special, when the spiritual truth is that we are all one. For today, let your inner guide step forward and lead you to open up to a new perspective.

Today's practice once again surrenders your ego's wrong perception to the right perception of your ~*ing*. When you choose your ~*ing* over your ego, you remember you are a spirit having a human experience and use your body as a learning device to deepen your spiritual faith.

■ Morning Reflection **DAY 17**

This morning, bring your passage to the mirror. Your work today is to read your morning passage out loud to yourself while looking in the mirror. When you're done reading your passage, look at yourself for one minute in the mirror.

> *This morning I call on my inner guide to help me see with new eyes. In this mirror I see my truth reflected back to me. I no longer hold a vision of my ego's fearful projections; I choose to see light instead. I see a beautiful ball of golden light above my head. This light pours over my body. The image of my body is covered in light.*

Affirmation Day 17

I AM NOT A BODY. I AM FREE.

Throughout the day when you recognize your ego's perception, come forward and simply say out loud: "I am not a body. I am free."

I find that when I say affirmations out loud, the words take on a higher power. Use this affirmation to plant a new miracle seed of intention.

You may not fully understand this concept at first—that's totally fine. If it's confusing to your ego, that's actually a good sign, because whatever is insane to the ego is sane to your ~ing. Fake it till you make it, and just let your ~ing take over.

■ Evening Exercise DAY 17

This evening I'll guide you in a meditation that introduces the *Course* lesson that inside each of us God placed a little spark of light. As we become more aware of the light within us, that light grows bigger and stronger. As it grows we begin to detach from our ego's projection of the body and awaken to our true light within. Let's begin the process by reigniting your light!

Follow my guided meditation passage here or visit www .gabbyb.tv/meditate for the audio download.

SPARK OF LIGHT MEDITATION

- Lie down in your bed with your palms facing upward.

- Take a deep breath in through your nose and exhale out your mouth.

- Continue this cycle of breath throughout your meditation.

- Envision in your heart a beautiful spark of golden light.

- As you breathe in, the light begins to shine brighter.

- On the exhale, it grows larger.

- Breathing in, envision the light shining brighter.

- On the exhale, the light grows larger.

- Continue this cycle of breath and enjoy the light show . . .

Day 18

GETTIN' MY GRATITUDE ON!

Today's practice will be another radical step toward achieving the miracle-minded perception of your body. You'll focus on what you love about your body, which will strengthen your right perceptions. Remember that the ego wants you to see your body as separate. Instead, today you will choose the miracle-minded perspective of seeing the body as equally as special as all other bodies through the practice of gratitude. Today's work will remind you of your body's true purpose: to be the embodiment of love and therefore a messenger for love. When you remember this, you can become grateful for your body and thereby disassociate from specialness, attack, and judgment. Gratitude for your body's true purpose awakens a new perception and releases all false illusions.

This is a really awesome part of the practice. When I began to put this principle into action, I intuitively started to love and care for my body more and release my ego's nasty beliefs. Miraculous shifts occur when you align your purpose with the desire to share love. So let's get you out of your own way and clear space for miracles!

■ Morning Passage **DAY 18**

This morning's reflection will be the catalyst for a transformational day. Sit comfortably in your meditation space and read the morning passage out loud to yourself. Then sit in stillness for one minute and let it marinate.

Today I accept the true purpose of my body. I am here to use this body as a learning device through which I become more connected to love. My physical healing offers me energy to be of higher service. I accept my body as vehicle for sharing more light with the world.

Affirmation Day 18

℘ I AM GRATEFUL FOR MY BODY.

Today's affirmation is accompanied by an exercise. Set aside some alone time and practice the following meditation.

During your lunch break sit comfortably (preferably alone) maybe in a park, at your desk, somewhere without distractions. Choose the most delicious bite of your meal and place it gently into your mouth. Think your affirmation in your mind, *I am grateful for my body.* Then spend one minute tasting (truly tasting) the food you have put in your mouth. Chew at least thirty times and let each flavor come forward. Experience the enjoyment of the delicious flavors and genuinely center into the present moment.

You can bring this exercise into all your physical experiences. When you go to the gym, take a moment to say, "I am grateful for my body" and spend one minute stretching your muscles deeper than you normally would. You can even bring this affirmation into your sex life. Often people become so disconnected from sexual experiences. This practice will help you connect again. Take this affirmation with you into your next sexual encounter and say to yourself (or out loud), "I am grateful for my body." Center into your body and enjoy sex in a whole new way. This affirmation and centering practice is designed to engage you in the present moment and enjoy the pleasures of life.

■ Evening Exercise **DAY 18**

Bust out your notebook for tonight's exercise. This work will deepen your understanding that the presence of fear is merely the absence of love. Though this may seem difficult to grasp at first, simply follow the exercise and get into the practice of seeing fear as False Evidence Appearing Real. Make a list of all the ways the ego's fear has affected your perception of your body. Next to each fearful projection, write the miracle-minded response.

Example 1:

> Fearful thought: *I am afraid I'll never lose weight and I feel disconnected from the world.*
> Miracle-minded response: *I recognize this fearful thought as my ego. I invite my inner guide to transform this thought and remind me that my body is love and I am one with the world.*

Example 2:

> Fearful thought: *I am addicted to food. I feel so empty that I must fill myself up with something. I will never overcome this addiction.*
>
> Miracle-minded response: *My addiction is fueled by fear. I surrender this addiction to the care of my inner guide and welcome support. I accept that I have chosen the ego's wrong perceptions and one moment at a time I choose differently.*

This exercise is not about trying to find the perfect response. You don't have to obsess over getting the words just right. Instead, it's about letting go and allowing your ~*ing* to come through in the writing process. The spirit of your inner guide always has a loving response. You just have to ask for help, and love will come through. So simply write out your fearful body perception and then invite your ~*ing* to respond.

To close out the day, before you go to sleep, read (or say out loud) the following prayer:

> *Inner Guide, I welcome your support. Thank you for leading me to the right perception of my body. Thank you for healing my false beliefs and addiction to fear. Thank you for reminding me of my body's purpose. Thank you for being my guide.*

Let this prayer guide you into a surrendered state. As you lie down to rest, let your ~*ing* come forward and do her thing. Let love pass through you and guide you in your sleep state. Let go, allow, and be guided.

Day 19

THE INVERSE OF THE FOG

Today we are throwin' down the F word once again. Forgiveness is the answer to releasing your ego's body fears and surrendering to miracles. Forgiveness helps shift from seeing our body as repulsive and bad to experiencing our bodies as love and light. Forgiveness will also help you let go of your anger, attack, and resentment toward yourself and others. The *Course* says: "If you give no power to the fog to obscure the light, it has none." This is the goal of today's work: to weaken the power we've given to the ego's fog and clear space for the light.

If you're carrying resentment toward someone who's abused your body, or if you're angry with yourself for inflicting your own pain, then forgiveness is imperative. If you remain unforgiving, you will re-create that negative experience over and over. When these experiences remain unhealed, the ego acts out to numb the past pain. Through forgiveness you can stop this ego behavior and set yourself free from the past. Even if you think you're not ready to forgive, allow today's practice to open you up to the possibility. Let's get the ball rolling with your morning reflection, and rock out with the F word.

■ Morning Reflection **DAY 19**

This morning's passage makes a statement to the Universe. It's likely that the act of forgiveness may seem very far from reach. Therefore, this morning's reflection will help you connect to the slight willingness to throw down the F word. Sit in your meditation space and take a moment to read your passage out loud to yourself. Then sit for one minute of stillness and let the words settle in.

> *Forgiveness heals my false perceptions of my body. Through forgiveness I restore my mind back to love. Today I no longer give power to the fog that has kept me in the dark. Instead I shine light on my body through forgiveness and awaken a new perspective.*

Affirmation Day 19

FORGIVENESS RESTORES MY PERCEPTION OF MY BODY BACK TO LOVE.

Through forgiveness you can unlearn your ego's behavior and restore your mind back to love. Today's affirmation will assist you in returning to your right perception of your body by awakening the desire to forgive. Remember that you're not alone in this process. Each time you say this affirmation, you're inviting your ~*ing* in for healing. So set your alarm to alert you three to five times a day and then recite at your Miracle Moments: "Forgiveness restores my perception of my body back to love."

Do not overthink this affirmation. Trust that by affirming this statement, you're igniting the forgiveness process, reinforcing faith in love, and lowering the ego's fog.

■ Evening Exercise DAY 19

This exercise embodies much of what the *Course* asks of its students: inviting their ~*ing* into the forgiveness process. One neat part of practicing the F word is that we're not expected to figure out how to forgive—all we need to do is bring our resentments to our ~*ing* and ask for loving guidance.

Our inner guide's forgiveness asks us to be willing to completely release all nonloving thoughts. However, our self-made "teacher," the ego, has made it seem quite dangerous to do this. To work past the ego's false perceptions, we must bring every secret that we've kept in the dark to our ~*ing* for healing. At our request, our ~*ing* will look on the darkness with us and lighten it away. Our inner guide will lead us to see that the hurt we felt was based on an incorrect interpretation. We will then learn that the darkness of our ego's pain cannot coexist with the light of our ~*ing*.

Today let's expose your ego's dark secrets to your ~*ing* so you can open up to forgiving yourself and your false perceptions. In this exercise, you will write a letter to your inner guide. Be open and honest about all the ways you've chosen your ego's false perception of your body. Tell your darkest secrets about your body and know that they are safe with your ~ing. You will ~ing-write this letter for ten minutes. Let your truth spill onto the page. Conclude the letter by asking your ~ing for guidance and support. Enjoy the cathartic process of releasing your secrets onto the page and trust that your ~ing has your back. Know that you're being guided.

The early evening exercise took you one big step closer to joining your thoughts with your ~ing. When you expose your secrets and ego to your inner guide, you weaken their strength. This in turn strengthens your faith in love, because you begin to see with your ~ing's perception rather than your ego's. The *Course* says: "Seeing with Him [your ~ing] will show you that all meaning, including yours, comes not from double vision, but from the gentle fusing of everything into one meaning, one emotion and one purpose." This is the point of the work we're doing together. The goal is to fuse your thoughts with the love of your ~ing so that love is all you choose to see.

Let's close out today's practice with another prayer to your inner guide. Read this prayer before you go to sleep:

> *Inner Guide, thank you for helping me release my fear. Thank you for guiding me to the right perception of my body. I choose to merge my thoughts with love. I forgive my fears and accept your guidance.*

Day 20

THE MIRACLE OF YOUR BODY

Let's start by acknowledging how much you rock! This week's work is a little ego mind-blowing and I honor you for hanging in there . . . so give yourself a big pat on the back and say "You did good!" All the work you've done this week has prepared you for today. I hope that today's work totally rocks your ego's world. The emphasis of each exercise today is on accepting your body's true function: to be love and extend love.

This work will push you far beyond your ego's comfort zone. That's a good thing! By accepting your body's true function, which is to be a messenger for love, you'll likely experience a miraculous shift. Remember that the miracle is a shift from body identification to spirit identification. Even for an instant you may come to realize that you're not here as a separate body among bodies, but rather as a spirit among spirits. When you turn to your ~ing for help, you will dissociate from the ego and be guided to use your body as a vehicle for sharing love with the world.

Accepting my body's true function has been instrumental

in my happiness and sense of purpose. Each time I get onstage to lead a lecture I say a prayer to my ~ing: "Inner Guide, please speak through me and use my body as a vehicle for love." This simple prayer reminds me that lecturing in front of hundreds of people is *not about me* but about being a messenger for love. As a result of asking my ~ing to speak through me, I become a vehicle for a loving message. I often don't remember what I say, my hands go numb, and I feel surges of energy pass through my body. My words flow freely, and I deeply connect to the audience. Through this simple prayer I am instantly reminded of my body's purpose and leave my ego backstage.

You too are a messenger for love. So let's start blasting light on your ego's body image!

■ Morning Reflection DAY 20

This morning's passage will set the tone for the rest of the day's exercises. For the sake of this exercise, let's light a candle to burn off your old beliefs and shine light on your path. Sit in your meditation space, light a candle, and read the following passage out loud. Then sit for one minute of stillness to let the love settle in.

> *Today I accept the true function of my body. I accept that my body is an instrument for extending love. As I heal my own perceptions of my body I will realize I am a vessel for sharing love with the world. My healing will be extended into the world.*

Affirmation Day 20

I ACCEPT THE TRUE FUNCTION OF MY BODY.
I ACCEPT THAT I AM A MESSENGER FOR LOVE.

Let's go big with today's affirmation. Set your Miracle Moment alarm for every hour on the hour. When the affirmation pops up on your phone or computer screen, take a moment to do the following:

- Breathe into your body and feel whatever feelings come over you.
- Say your affirmation out loud or in your mind.
- Take another deep breath in and see if there is an emotional shift.
- Write down exactly how you're feeling after you say this affirmation.

This exercise is invaluable because it helps you pay attention to how your affirmations can proactively shift your energy. If even the slightest bit of energy shifts within you, it's a miracle. Pay attention to the power of each intention you put forward. As you become more and more accepting of the purpose of your body, you will experience many energetic shifts. Pay attention to the miracles.

■ Evening Exercise **DAY 20**

The affirmation exercise was meant to show you how you can shift your energy when you connect to your purpose. This evening's exercise reinforces the belief that when you think with positivity and love's purpose, you can recalibrate your energy and be relieved from the ego's strife. To take this exercise one step further, I invite you to do another breathing exercise with your affirmation. We will use the mantra "I accept the true function of my body. I accept that I am a messenger for love."

- Breathe in: *I accept the true function of my body.*

- Breathe out: *I accept that I am a messenger for love.*

- Breathe in: *I accept the true function of my body.*

- Breathe out: *I accept that I am a messenger for love.*

- Breathe in: *I accept the true function of my body.*

- Breathe out: *I accept that I am a messenger for love.*

Continue this breathing exercise for five minutes. When you're done, write down in your journal how you feel. You can also acknowledge any other thoughts that come through. Let your -ing come forward, and plant your subconscious mind onto the page.

Day 21

REFLECT AND PREPARE

Let's conclude the week's exercises with self-reflection and preparation.

■ **Morning Reflection DAY 21**

Reread your exercises from this week. Be very proud of the work you've done. Our ego's false perception of the body is tough to overcome. One day at a time you'll come to know a new truth. One of my favorite teachers, Thich Nhat Hanh, said, "People have a hard time letting go of their suffering. Out of fear of the unknown, they prefer suffering that is familiar." Take this in and acknowledge yourself for stepping into the unknown and awakening your miracle mind-set.

■ **Evening Exercise DAY 21**

This week's practice will greatly serve you as we move into Week Four. Before bed, read the introduction to Week Four and prepare to bring miracles into your relationships. Remember that your body is a tool for spiritual growth and expansion. Use your body as an expression of love and your relationships will shift dramatically. Enjoy the miracles.

WEEK 4

RELATIONSHIPS

You practice loving God by loving another human.

—Olivia Harrison

I can safely say that the majority of the people who read my books or attend my lectures do so because of a tripped-up relationship. Whether it's with a business partner, a romantic partner, a family member, or a past lover, rocky relationships are where the ego really goes to town.

Ego-based relationships are nightmares. When your relationships are run by fear, all kinds of crazy stuff comes up: jealousy, judgment, attack, anger, and unnecessary resentment. As you learned in Week Three, the ego uses the body to create more separation in our relationships to others. When you perceive yourself as a separate body, inevitably you've projected yourself as better than or less than someone else—this is what the *Course* calls the "special relationship." The special relationship is based on seeing others as separate and different. Typically we think "special" is a good thing. In this case, the concept of special implies that we're better or less than others, which heightens our faith in separation from oneness. In the special relationship, judgment, attack, idolizing, and comparing are at an all-time high. Whether you're judging the other person or judging yourself, you're experiencing the same ego nightmare. In fact, the *Course* teaches that judging others is the same thing as judging yourself. Since the *Course's* perspective is that we are all one, judging someone else *is* judging everyone—including you.

We all make special relationships in many ways. We have the special friend relationship with the person we perceive as our best friend—we have very high expectations of this person. Then there's the special parent relationship, in which we make an idol of a parent and will always need to live up to their expectations (or what we perceive to be their expectations). In the special work relationship, we place our boss or a coworker on a pedestal and need their approval and validation to feel good enough. (Alternatively, we make ourselves more special than those we employ.) These are just a few examples of how the ego's specialness creates separation.

And then there's the big one—the McSpecial with a side of fries, the ego's nastiest trick of all: the special love relationship. I bet you know this all too well: the romantic partner you thought was the answer to your problems, the key to your happiness . . . only to end in a tortured breakup that you replay in your mind for more than a decade. Sound familiar? Okay, maybe I'm being a bit dramatic, but it's more likely I'm spot-on. Either way, I know we've all experienced this kind of ego torture in some way, because romantic love is the ego's ace of spades.

The special love relationship is the trippiest of all special relationships, because the ego convinces us that this one special person will save us. The ego substitutes the divine love within us with the special love relationship we've seen in movies or magazines. The special love relationship is based on the premise that something outside of us can fill up or compensate for what seems to be lacking inside. Replacing our inner presence of power and love with one special idol will always be false. But recognizing the presence of love within offers us real power. The ego's world teaches that there is separation between all special relationships—the special friend love, special romantic love, special family love, and special work love. The ego can give love to one person and deny another entirely. This ego mentality is a spiral that deepens the dissociation from God's one love and heightens faith in separation.

Special love is based on dependency and lack. The ego convinces us that we're alone, which leads us to desperately seek completion in others. This experience of lack grows out of our profound sense of separation from our real spiritual identity. Believing this state of lack to be our reality, we seek special relationships to help us feel whole. Regardless of how hard we try, we never actually achieve that feeling of wholeness, because special love creates chaos and division. Our special love relationships lead us to jealousy, envy, and a constant state of fear of abandonment. This relationship is based on neurotic, fearful romance that can be the ego's chief weapon for keeping us in the dark. For instance, maybe your ego has convinced you that you're not good enough without your special partner. This belief makes you extremely fearful of losing your one special love, and therefore you are always controlling the relationship to keep it intact. You may lash out in a jealous rage when your partner talks to someone else, or maybe you constantly worry whether the person is really in love with you. The special relationship can make us crazy in all kinds of ways. It can put us at war with each other as we project our fear onto our special partner.

Thinking that you'll find all your happiness in the arms of a special partner will always disappoint you. Special love will never work—period. Think about it this way: What happens when the special idol ends the relationship? Your source of happiness and salvation ends, and your ego convinces you

you're unsafe. This pattern happens far too often and is one of the ego's greatest tricks for keeping us in the darkness.

The ego is very unforgiving in relationships. When the ego perceives attack, its response is to immediately attack back. This type of ego pattern can go on for years—even a lifetime. If we're unaware of our ego's fear, forgiveness is a distant afterthought. Therefore, we stay stuck in the pattern of attack, thinking that we're protecting ourselves from being hurt. But in truth, we're only protecting the ego. When we hold on to past resentments in new relationships, we replay the negativity and rehearse the role of victim on a daily basis. To make matters worse, we carry that same resentment into new experiences, placing blame and doubt onto more innocent people. The ego's need to be right in all situations drains our energy and keeps us stuck in a cycle of fearful illusion.

I have learned many great lessons that have reinforced that happiness always trumps being right. One example is based on a special relationship I created with a teacher whom I really respect and admire. I idolized this person in an unhealthy way. This person said something about me in public that upset me greatly. My immediate response was to go into self-protection mode and attack back. I called several friends to complain, I cried, and then I swore I'd never speak to her again. Though I didn't directly attack her with my words or actions, I had her in a headlock with my attack thoughts. This internal drama went on for weeks.

As a miracle worker, I'm well aware of how the ego reacts to the feeling of being attacked. The *Course* teaches that the ego speaks first and loudest, squashing and silencing reason. In this case, my ego was at the front line with a megaphone and a sledgehammer. This ego reaction totally took me down. As time wore on I began to pay attention to the way this resentment was affecting my energy and my happiness. My need to be right held me back from any chance of forgiveness and release.

A *Course in Miracles* asks, "Would you rather be right or happy?" Clearly, the loving response is to choose happiness over the ego's need to be right—but happiness can be hard to achieve when you believe you've been deeply wronged.

A lack of forgiveness hurts us in nasty ways. When the ego blocks us from forgiving, we inevitably take on certain fearful archetypes. Here are some of the personality traits we pick up from the ego's unforgiving ways.

The Daily Victim: When we're unwilling to forgive, we wake up each day feeling like a victim. We hold tight to our past hurt and resentment, replaying it in our mind over and over again. This automatic replay reinforces the ego's illusion and strengthens our perception of being the victim. Eventually we identify so closely with the role of victim that we begin to establish that dynamic in all our relationships.

The Angry Boxer: When the ego feels attacked, its immediate response is to attack back. The ego has faith in fear and believes that we're at the mercy of a cruel world. So it keeps its boxing gloves slung over the shoulder, always on alert to fight off an attack. These defensive thoughts and energy bleed off the angry boxer and inevitably create more negative experiences. It's a wicked cycle.

The Shutdown and Protected: This is the person whose ego has convinced them to shut themselves off from the world for fear of being hurt again. The shutdown person lives small, hides out, and evades all potential conflict by avoiding intimacy altogether.

These are just a few of the many ways the ego's lack of forgiveness holds us back in relationships. Letting go of our need to be right and surrendering to forgiveness is the only way out of the ego's unforgiving nightmare. If we truly want to enjoy our relationships, we must respect them through the miraculous act of forgiveness.

A *Course in Miracles* suggests we use this affirmation: "I could see peace instead of this." When we choose for peace, we'll put down the boxing gloves, come out of hiding, and throw down the F word. The process of forgiveness requires willingness to see things differently. The *Course* doesn't suggest we pretend like nothing happened—rather, that we acknowledge our ego's experience and choose to perceive it with love.

A daily practice of willingness is our greatest guide to truthful forgiveness and release. Another powerful affirmation for reinforcing the forgiveness process is to say, "I'd rather be happy than right." Choosing happiness is always the path of least resistance. When you confirm your commitment to happiness, you weaken your faith in resentment.

Finally, it's important to commit to releasing the victim mentality. If you honestly want to release your resentment, you have to no longer want to be the victim. We often get caught in the role of victim because the ego thrives on it. Getting out of this role requires a commitment to see things differently. If you're the angry victim, try this powerful prayer from the

Course: "I am not the victim of the world I see." Whenever you notice yourself getting caught up in victimhood, simply say this prayer and gently remind yourself that you'd rather be happy.

Choosing happiness is a full-time job. We have many obstacles that get in the way of our peace, so we must commit to letting go of petty resentments, a victim mentality, and fear. We must surrender to love.

I took these steps into my forgiveness practice and surrendered to the willingness to be happy rather than right. After a week of full-blown surrender, I experienced a quantum shift. In my morning meditation I began to think about the teacher I'd been resenting. In that instant, an overwhelming sense of love came out of nowhere. My inner guide led me to call on love and experience a tremendous sense of gratitude. In that moment I released her. I cried with joy as I let go of the petty resentment and opened my heart to forgiveness.

Then ten minutes later I checked my e-mail. There was a message in my in-box from that same teacher! In the same instant that I released her, she sent a loving e-mail acknowledging how proud she was of me. I laughed at the little wink from the Universe and I relished in the miracle. Love has the power to transform any situation; you just have to choose to be happy rather than right.

This story about my teacher offers up a great example of the unholy relationship transformed to love. *A Course in Miracles* dedicates ten chapters of the text (Chapters 15–24) to transforming the ego's unholy relationship into a *holy relationship* through the practice of forgiveness. The holy relationship is the ego's unholy relationship transformed through forgiveness and love. When you restore your mind back to love, reconnect to oneness, and release the ego's separation, the holy relationship sets in. This requires a serious commitment to the miracles and a whole lot of surrender.

Every relationship offers you the opportunity to grow toward holy love. The *Course* emphasizes how every encounter is a holy encounter because every relationship offers us the opportunity to transcend the ego's false perception and move past the unholy relationship. Your relationship to a cabdriver, an intern, a volunteer, a family member, or a lover are all equal opportunities for you to make the relationship not about conflict, separation, and fear—but rather, love. The ego is present in every encounter, but the *Course* suggests that we use relationships as learning devices for overturning the ego's false perceptions.

To transform a relationship from unholy to holy, you must change the intention for the relationship.

The intention of the ego is to maintain control over the perception that the other person is separate, through attack, judgment, jealousy, and so on. The ego uses fear to keep the cheap drama alive within a relationship. When the ego's goal is to maintain control over the relationship, your thoughts steer far away from forgiveness and acceptance, and the boxing gloves come out. When your ego is driving the relationship, you can be sure to think crazy thoughts and do crazy things. The ego convinces us that we're "protecting" ourselves by thinking attack thoughts toward our partner, when in effect we're actually creating more attack.

The miracle worker's intention is quite the opposite. When the goal of the relationship is to find peace and love, a much different experience occurs. When you follow the miracle worker's goal for relationships, you're guided to surrender your fear to your inner guide for correction. You're not expected to just let go of the ego overnight. But much like all the exercises in this book, the simple solution to the ego's special relationship is to turn it over to your ~ing for healing. This spiritual act of surrender releases you from the ego's grip and opens up your consciousness to receive guidance. When I find the ego making special relationships difficult, I invite my inner guide to act as the invisible intermediary whose goal is to bring the connection back to love. Though this may be hard for your ego to accept, the purpose will become clear. Your ~ing shifts the goal of the relationship from one in which you defend specialness and separation to one in which you experience oneness and wholeness. Your inner guide will lead you to a new purpose of the relationship.

It's important to be mindful that the ego will be uncomfortable with the miracle worker's goal. As it says in the *Course*, "As these two contemplate their relationship from the point of view of this new purpose, they are inevitably appalled. Their perception of the relationship may even become quite disorganized. And yet, the former organization of their perception no longer serves the purpose they have agreed to meet." When you invite love to intervene in your unholy relationship, the ego will go to town. The ego believes that to be safe in relationships you must stay in control. Therefore, expect some ego backlash as I open you up this week to work in relationships, and expect many miraculous shifts.

The shifts that occur result in what the *Course* refers to as the "holy instant": the moment you let go of the ego's drama. When you both join in this holy union, letting love host the relationship rather than the ego, the relationship can be very enjoyable. You will feel a sense of relief and freedom. But even though *you* may experience a holy instant, the other person may resist. If the other is dependent on the ego's perception of the relationship, then he or she will likely be uncomfortable with your change. This happens often. Think about those times in your life when you were willing to grow and your partner was not. When that happens, the romantic relationship ends and the form of the relationship changes. People tend to get distraught when relationships change in form—but actually, it's fine. A breakup (romantic or otherwise) can be the biggest drama for the ego. But from the *Course*'s perspective, these changes occur naturally when you're committed to love. If the form of a relationship changes through forgiveness, you may feel sad, but you've still received the gift: spiritual growth. The relationship offered you an opportunity to choose your ~*ing*'s perception over your ego. When you choose to let love host your relationship, it doesn't matter whether you stay or go—all that matters is your internal shift toward love. This is when the relationship is made holy in your mind.

Bringing love into all your relationships will dramatically change your life. I've recently undergone a miraculous transformation in this area. I've been a student of the *Course* for seven years, so I've become accustomed to witnessing my ego in action. A regular practice of outing your ego is key to being a miracle worker. For years I've practiced outing my ego each time I'd focus on separation rather than oneness. I found that I was great at applying the *Course*'s principles of forgiveness in relationships that were really important to me, but I was less likely to consider the F word and oneness in relationships I perceived as "less significant." I saw certain relationships as more important or at the forefront of my life, while others were not as present. For instance, in my romantic arena I proudly practiced the F word every day, consciously supporting a holy love relationship. But in certain business relationships or connections to people I met briefly on the street, I was less likely to throw down the F word and practice oneness. Upon realizing this, I turned to my ~*ing* for help. I asked my inner guide to help me bring an equal amount of loving intentions to all my relationships and to help me be more egalitarian with my perceptions.

Outing my ego to my ~*ing* never fails to restore my miracle mind-set. When I bring my ego to my ~*ing* for healing, I'm often guided to open *A Course in Miracles* for the solution. The same day I asked for help, I opened the text of the *Course* to this passage: "Even at the level of the most casual encounter is the possibility for two people to lose sight of separate interests if only for a moment. That moment will be enough." The message couldn't have been clearer. My inner guide had nailed it once again. I was to practice love and forgiveness "even at the level of the most casual encounter." Though I perceived myself as deeply connected to the *Course*, I had still missed a major step: to practice these principles in all my affairs. Once again I was led to a new opportunity to invite my ~*ing* to lead the way. My inner guide always has my back.

I bring up this story to inspire you as you begin your miracle-minded practice in relationships. This week, don't just dedicate the work to one special relationship that's been driving you nuts. Instead, I encourage you to apply this week's exercises to all the relationships in your life—even those that last only for a few minutes. A stranger on the street, a cashier in a shop, or a chance encounter in an airport all offer you an ego nightmare or holy bliss. It's your choice. So be prepared to work with all kinds of relationships this week, and do not emphasize one special relationship.

Throughout this week we're going to blast through more fear and raise your miracle-minded consciousness to awesome new heights. Outlined next is a breakdown of what you can expect!

- On **Day 22**, you'll pay attention to what you think about others. This is an exercise in getting clear about how the ego has convinced you of separation. This work will help you see that even when you treat people kindly, if your thoughts don't match your actions, you're still caught up in ego warfare. The goal for this day is to become highly aware of how the ego separates and makes special.
- The exercises on **Day 23** are geared toward surrendering your ego to your ~*ing* for healing. From the seemingly insignificant to the most important relationships in your life, you will be guided to let your ~*ing* lead the ego to the light. You'll learn how the ego needs darkness to hide—but if you're willing to call on the light of your ~*ing*, you'll be able to transform your relationships. This practice will not rely on the participation of someone else. Just invite spirit into all your relationships, and your experience of each relationship will change.
- The practice on **Day 24** is based on this lesson from the *Course* workbook: "Kindness created me kind."

This affirmation reminds us that we came from a loving, kind place; the way we will return there is to act with kindness. The exercises through this day will guide you to practice the affirmation *Kindness created me kind* whenever the ego attacks others.

- The practice on **Day 25** will help you understand the principle that what we project onto others we reflect back onto ourselves. The *Course* teaches us that the thoughts we have about others are a mirror reflection of the thoughts we believe to be real about ourselves. Through the practice of gratitude you'll be guided to clean up your thoughts about others and in effect heal your thoughts about yourself.

- The practice on **Day 26** helps you understand how the ego uses forgiveness to get what it wants, whereas your ~ing uses forgiveness to return to love. This work will also guide you to understand a powerful principle from the *Course*, which is that through forgiveness you can choose oneness no matter what has been said or done.

- On **Day 27**, you'll be guided to pay attention to the holy instant. Each time you shift your perception from separation to oneness you'll document the experience. Throughout the day, as you practice bringing love to all your relationships, you will enjoy the feelings that pass over you.

- As always, the last day of each week is dedicated to a review of the week's work and preparation for the week to come. On **Day 28** you will recap and then prepare for Week Five by reading the introduction.

This week's work will reinforce one of the primary principles of this practice: that all thinking produces form on some level. Each thought you have directly affects the way you experience your life. As you start to change the way you think about relationships, the way you experience them will change. Letting go of negativity and resentment will help you see more oneness and love in everyone. You will no longer feel comfortable judging, comparing, attacking, and gossiping. You'll intuitively want to feel a more loving connection with everyone you meet. It's much more enjoyable to live the loving way in relationships. Follow the guided steps and expect miracles.

Day 22

WITNESS YOUR EGO'S SPECIAL ILLUSIONS

Today you'll be guided to pay attention to what you think about others. This is an exercise in getting clear about how the ego has convinced you of separation. As you know by now, clarity is king when overcoming the ego's mad ideas. The more aware you are of your ego's beliefs, the easier it will be to decide to change your mind. Today's goal is to become highly aware of how the ego separates us from others and makes people special. We become comfortable in the ego's perception of others, using attack and judgment to "protect" ourselves from being hurt or disappointed. Today's practice will challenge the ego's crafty tricks and show you how separation interferes with your happiness. Witnessing your ego's separation is the first step toward reconnecting with peace and oneness in all relationships.

Trust that this week's work will challenge your ego's perceptions. Therefore, it's important to set down a solid foundation for the work. By fearlessly witnessing your ego in action, you'll begin the process of transforming the ego's false beliefs.

■ Morning Reflection **DAY 22**

Get comfortable in your meditation space. Read the passage that follows out loud to yourself and then take a deep breath in and release. Sit in stillness for one minute to let the words set in.

> *Today I commit to witnessing my ego's false perceptions of others. I invite my inner guide to help me see how I have wrongly judged others. I will become aware of how I've compared myself to others, attacked, and made people more special and separate than me. I will be the witness to my ego's false beliefs, and I welcome the process of undoing this behavior.*

Affirmation Day 22

TODAY I AM THE WITNESS TO MY EGO'S FALSE PERCEPTIONS OF OTHERS.

Once again, let's reaffirm your goal: to witness your ego's misperceptions. Today's practice is to witness how you judge, attack, compare, and make others more special or less special. Each time you witness these behaviors, you can use your affirmation and bring your negativity to your ~*ing* for healing. Witnessing your ego in action is the first step toward bringing the false projection to your ~*ing* for healing.

At this point in your practice, you no longer need to use your alarm as a reminder to say your affirmation (though you can if you choose). Your miracle mind-set is on, so you're ready to practice becoming mindful of your thoughts toward others. Each time you catch your ego judging, attacking, making special idols, and disconnecting from oneness, simply say your affirmation: "Today I am the witness to my ego's false perceptions of others."

■ Evening Exercise **DAY 22**

This evening, take out your notebook and make a list of five ways you separated yourself from others today. In what ways did you choose the ego's false beliefs and see separation rather than oneness? Answer the following questions:

1. How do I judge others?
2. How do I attack others (in my mind or through my actions)?
3. Whom do I make special?
4. How do I make myself more special than others?
5. How do I compare myself to others?

After writing your answers, say a silent prayer:

> *Inner Guide, I am aware of my ego's false beliefs and no longer choose this path. I welcome you to help me heal these fearful ways and guide me toward oneness with all.*

Before bed, close your day with another prayer, which will set you up for the day to come:

> *I witness how I have chosen to deny love. I witness how I have made others special. I choose love instead of this. Inner Guide, lead the way.*

Day 23

BE WILLING TO TURN YOUR EGO OVER TO YOUR ~ING

Good morning, miracle worker. Today we're going to rock out a full-blown surrender. By now you know the main way to heal your ego's false perceptions is to invite in the spirit of your inner guide for help. When you surrender, you invite your inner guide to intervene in the relationship. When you release your ego to your ~ing, you'll feel the presence of a silent companion whose primary purpose is to guide you to forgive. Welcome this guidance, and trust that through forgiveness you will reconnect with oneness and peace.

This step cannot be skipped. If you're unwilling to let your ~ing enter into the relationship, you will not be conscious of the guidance around you. Your willingness awakens your consciousness.

■ Morning Reflection **DAY 23**

Our goal for today is to create powerful shifts in your dedication to the work. Therefore, let's begin with a morning passage that will set you up to win for the day. Get comfortable in your meditation space and read the following passage out loud. Then sit in one minute of stillness and allow your inner guide to come forward.

> *Inner Guide, I call on you for help. I know I have chosen separation over oneness and fear over love. For today, I choose to see everyone as equal and release my fears to your care. I wholeheartedly welcome your guidance. I ask that you teach me to perceive everyone as equal, and to see everyone as love. Teach me love through every holy encounter.*

Affirmation Day 23

INNER GUIDE, I ASK THAT YOU HELP ME SEE EVERYONE AS EQUAL.

You'll use today's affirmation frequently throughout the day. Each encounter you have with another person offers you an opportunity to invite your ~*ing*'s perception to come forward. Rather than let your ego meddle in your encounters, say your affirmation and invite your ~*ing* in from the get-go.

Each time you ask your ~*ing* to help you see oneness over separation, you're choosing your ~*ing*'s vision instead of your ego's. The more you call on love, the more love you will see. The goal is to let your ~*ing* replace your ego's unholy relationship and restore your loving mind.

■ Evening Exercise **DAY 23**

This evening's exercise will expand on yesterday's work. Answer the same questions that follow. It's likely that many of your answers will be similar to the day before. The difference today is that you're going to respond to your ego with love.

Answer the following questions in your journal and then respond by saying out loud: "I am willing to see love instead of this."

1. How did I judge others today?
   Response: "I am willing to see love instead of this."
2. How did I attack others today (in my mind or actions)?
   Response: "I am willing to see love instead of this."
3. Whom did I make special today?
   Response: "I am willing to see love instead of this."
4. How did I make myself more special today?
   Response: "I am willing to see love instead of this."
5. How did I compare myself to others today?
   Response: "I am willing to see love instead of this."

This evening, close your day with a willingness meditation. Read the meditation here or visit www.gabbyb.tv/meditate for the audio version.

WILLINGNESS MEDITATION

- Get comfortable in your meditation space.
- Sit up straight with your palms facing upward.

- Take a deep breath in through your nose and exhale out through your mouth.

- Continue this cycle of breath throughout your meditation.

- Breathe in: *I am willing to surrender my ego to my inner guide.*

- Breathe out: *I am ready to let go of my false perceptions.*

- Breathe in: *I am willing to see oneness in all.*

- Breathe out: *I am ready to see love.*

- Breathe in: *I am willing to surrender my ego to my inner guide.*

- Breathe out: *I am ready to let go of my false perceptions.*

- Breathe in: *I am willing to see oneness in all.*

- Breathe out: *I am ready to see love.*

- Continue repeating these affirmations as you breathe in and out.

- When you're ready, open your eyes to the room.

Enjoy your sleep this evening knowing that your *~ing* is working with you even while you dream.

Day 24

KINDNESS CREATED ME KIND

Today's exercises are based on this passage from the *Course* workbook: "Kindness created me kind." This message reminds us that we came from a loving, kind place and that through thoughts of kindness we will remember our truth. Let love enter into your mind even more, and make kindness your primary goal today. Enjoy the beautiful experience of genuine altruism and authentic love.

■ Morning Reflection DAY 24

Today's morning passage will remind you of who you truly are: a being of love. I suggest that you look in the mirror as you read this passage out loud to yourself. Sit in front of a mirror and read the passage out loud as you gaze gently at your reflection:

Kindness created me kind. I come from love and kindness, and I know this is who I am. Today I choose to remember my truth and share it with the world. Today I will spread loving-kindness to all those I encounter.

Affirmation Day 24

KINDNESS CREATED ME KIND.

> Throughout the day, witness when your ego attacks others. In these moments use your affirmation, "Kindness created me kind." Don't overthink anything; just let the words remind you of your truth and guide you to release the attack thought. Use your affirmation whenever judgment, separation, or attack set in.

■ Evening Exercise DAY 24

From the *Course's* perspective, if kindness created you, then being unkind disconnects you from your truth. When we witness our unkind thoughts and actions, we know we're not connected to the truthful state from which we came. Though you may perceive yourself as a kind person, one unkind thought or action knocks you out of your alignment to love.

Even the kindest people judge and attack others in their minds. Unless you're an enlightened master, it's likely that no matter how hard you try to be kind, the ego will sneak in somewhere. That's fine. Now that you're on the miracle-minded path, your subtle shifts will awaken your awareness of where you can grow and learn. This evening's exercise will do just that:

1. Make a list of the ways you have been unkind this week. Whether through your thoughts or actions, how have you disconnected from your truth?

2. Take a moment to reflect on the list and describe in your journal how it feels to be unkind.

3. The final step is to forgive yourself for your unkind thoughts and actions. Say the following prayer out loud:

I recognize how I've been unkind. I acknowledge that this behavior is not who I truly am. I now know that this unkindness comes from my ego's wrong decision to choose fear over love. I forgive myself for this wrong-minded decision. I choose to see love instead.

You can take these three steps into your day-to-day life. Each time you witness yourself being unkind, take a moment to reflect on how it makes you feel—and then immediately forgive yourself. By continuously acknowledging your unkind ego behavior, you will weaken the bad habit and transcend the ego's need to judge.

Day 25

BE GRATEFUL FOR THE PURPOSE OF THE RELATIONSHIP

Today's practice will help you understand a crucial principle: What we project onto others we reflect back onto ourselves. The *Course* teaches us that the thoughts we have about others are a mirror reflection of the thoughts we believe to be real about ourselves. For instance, if you find yourself judging others for being overweight, it's likely you have issues with your own weight or appearance. Or you may find that in your mind you attack people who are in happy relationships. It's possible that this attack is merely a reflection of your own desire to have that type of romantic love. When you place judgment or blame on or attack others, there is often an unconscious sense of lack stemming from within you. Through the practice of gratitude, you'll be guided to clean up your thoughts about others, thereby healing your thoughts about yourself. When we send love toward what we want, we feel better about ourselves and thereby experience more love in our own life. Gratitude creates a domino effect of love.

But we're not stopping there. Many of us carry past resentments toward others for decades. For instance, one of my clients lost her job in 2008 when the recession first hit. It took her more than two years to find another job. Through her spiritual practice she came to understand that the resentment and fear she had about losing her last job was greatly affecting her ability to get another job. Each time she went on an interview she'd attack and judge herself for fear of not being liked. This energy held her back from getting a new job. Through her miracle-minded practice she was able to become grateful for the lessons she learned on the old job, and she chose to let go of the fear from the past. She accepted the learning opportunity that had been given to her.

Today's work will help you accept all your relationships as assignments for spiritual growth. When you accept this truth, you become grateful for the lessons you have learned. In turn, you recognize how the lessons carry you to the next level of faith in miracles.

■ **Morning Reflection DAY 25**

Today's morning reflection will help you begin the day by seeing your most difficult relationships as assignments for learning and growth. Beginning your day with this attitude will help you infuse all your encounters with love.

Get comfortable in your meditation space and read the passage that follows, then sit for one minute of stillness as the message settles in.

Today I perceive all my relationships as assignments. I choose
to see each encounter as an opportunity for spiritual growth.
I am grateful for the lessons these relationships bring.

Affirmation Day 25

ALL ENCOUNTERS ARE HOLY ENCOUNTERS.

This affirmation is one of the most transformational statements in this book. Throughout the day (and hopefully for the rest of your life), use this affirmation in all ego encounters. When you sense yourself disconnecting from love in the presence of others, remind yourself that *all encounters are holy encounters*. In other words, every person you meet offers you the opportunity to strengthen your miracle mind-set through the choice to perceive love over fear. This affirmation is a gentle reminder to perceive each encounter as an assignment to see love instead of fear. Bringing this affirmation into each encounter will get you into the subtle practice of creating oneness in all your relationships regardless of the ego's preconceived notions.

Bonus Exercise: Release Special Love

The thought that one person can be your source of inspiration, excitement, and bliss is a pipe dream. Rather than seek romance in one special love partner, open up to the possibility for more fiery sparks within your friendships. When you ignite more excitement and fun in your friendly relationships, you put less pressure on your romantic partner. This is a powerful tool for creating more oneness in the ego's most challenging relationship of all, romantic love.

This week, go on a date with a friend. The goal of this date is to recognize how fulfilling friendships can be. Enjoy your friend's company in a whole new way by focusing the same attention on the friendship as you would with a romantic partner. Okay, so you won't be making out with your best friend—but you can be equally inspired by their personality and unique traits. By perceiving your friendship as more "romantic," you'll increase a sense of companionship and oneness.

The benefit of shifting your perspective in friendship is not only that you have more fun, but that you let romantic partners off the hook. By bringing more romance into your friendships, you no longer need a romantic partner to be your only source of happiness. This shift guides you to radiate a more confident energy and release neediness and lack.

Set yourself free from the false perception that one special person will save you. Create more oneness by igniting fiery sparks in all your relationships!

■ **Evening Exercise DAY 25**

Tonight, spend some time reflecting on your day. Write down three ways your affirmation served you and helped you shift your perceptions from ego to holiness. Acknowledge your shifts.

End your day with what I call a Holy Instant Meditation. This awesome meditation will help you release unholy projections and welcome in love.

HOLY INSTANT MEDITATION

- Get comfortable in your meditation space.
- Begin your meditative breathing.

- Breathe in through your nose and out through your mouth.

- Continue this cycle of breath throughout the meditation.

- As you continue to breathe, think for a moment of someone whom you recently judged.

- Regardless of how well you know this person, allow his or her image to enter into your mind's eye.

- Breathe in all the feelings that come up.

- On the exhale, release.

- Continue breathing deeper and deeper into the experience .

- In the discomfort of this feeling, invite your ~ing in for healing.

- Breathe in: *Inner Guide, I need your help.*

- Breathe out: *I am willing to see love instead of this.*

- Upon saying this prayer, witness a beautiful blanket of golden light melt over your body.

- This blanket of light is cleansing you of judgment and clearing you of all attack.

- Breathe in this golden light.

- Breathe out a sigh of release.

- See this same blanket of light pour over the person whom you have judged.

- See the light cleanse your perception of this person.

- Eventually all you see is light.

- Recognize in this holy instant that the light in you is a reflection of the light in them.

- You are one in the light.

Day 26

F EVERYONE!

The practice today will help you understand how the ego denies forgiveness to get what it wants—whereas ~ing uses forgiveness to reconnect to love. What's the difference? The ego's goal is to maintain the illusion of fear, because if the illusion is exposed, the ego will have no purpose. Therefore, the ego will always be unwilling to forgive. This unwillingness keeps the dark illusion alive. But your ~ing's goal is much different. Your inner guide uses forgiveness as the primary tool for restoring your faith in love. Forgiveness is the answer to true serenity and peace.

This work will also guide you to understand a powerful principle from the *Course*, which is that through forgiveness you can choose oneness . . . no matter what has been said or done. For instance, a coaching client of mine had been deeply betrayed by her father at a young age when he left her family without any money or support. The pain from the experience led her ego to project fear onto all her relationships. She lived in fear that she was unlovable and therefore attacked everyone to "protect" herself from being hurt again. Through her practice of forgiveness she was able to fully forgive and release her father. The result of this forgiveness was that she then began a practice of regular forgiveness in all her relationships. Forgiveness offered her a clean slate for all new relationships to begin with the perception of oneness and love. As a result of her relaxed, forgiving state, she energetically began to attract more loving, kind people who would never betray her. It's also important to point out that she was able to fully forgive her father without ever having to see him. You don't have to be face-to-face to forgive, because forgiveness happens on a spiritual level and affects your physical perception of the world.

Again I ask, would you rather be right or happy? Clearly the miracle worker's response is to choose happiness over the ego's need to be right, though it can be difficult to do. Letting go of our need to be right and surrendering to forgiveness is one of the primary principles of this week's work. If we're to truly enjoy our relationships, we must respect them through the miraculous act of forgiveness.

■ Morning Reflection DAY 26

Get comfortable in your meditation space and prepare for today's practice. Today's spiritual food will whet your mental appetite for the miracle of forgiveness. Each thought you have will let your ~ing guide you to see love and peace instead of fear. Read the following passage and allow your ~ing to lead the way. Then sit for one minute of stillness and let your mind and spirit absorb the words.

Today I will create the holy instant through the practice of forgiveness. With each holy encounter, I choose to forgive and release my ego's false projections. Forgiveness reminds me that we are one. Each time I have a false attack thought toward someone, I will choose to forgive the thought and remember that we are one. In turn, I forgive myself.

Affirmation Day 26

I COULD SEE PEACE INSTEAD OF THIS.

Throughout the day, use this affirmation as a guide to opening your heart to love and peace with each and every encounter. This affirmation helps you release judgment of your ego's false perceptions and forgive them instead. It also reminds you that with each encounter, you have a choice: the choice to see peace. Each encounter is a new opportunity to use your affirmation and choose to see love. *Remember that your inner guide is all love and never judges your practice.* Today's affirmation will reinforce this faith by forgiving all attack thoughts toward others.

■ Evening Exercise **DAY 26**

This evening's work will help you release your false projections of others through a forgiveness meditation. Some of my greatest acts of forgiveness have occurred on my meditation pillow. When we invite spirit into the forgiveness process, we can let go of our grievances and allow love to cleanse the ego's dark illusions. Trust that today's exercises have awakened your desire to forgive and that love has been called.

Today's work was no small feat. It's not easy to forgive your attack thoughts and choose to see love in everyone. It's likely this work has led to your ego flipping out. There's nothing wrong with that—just allow your ego to be present with you in the midst of this transition and trust that the more you become faithful to love, the less patience you'll have for your ego. To-night we will close this powerful day with a prayer, which you can read silently or out loud to yourself:

> *Thank you, Inner Guide, for helping me forgive my ego's false perceptions. I welcome you always as my teacher to remind me that every encounter is a holy encounter and to choose forgiveness as my guide back to love and peace.*

Day 27

MIRACULOUS RELATIONSHIPS

Today you'll be guided to pay attention to the holy instant. Through your miracle-minded perspective you'll be guided to release old fears and restore your faith in oneness: this is the holy instant. Enjoy the metamorphosis that occurs when you let love in. Each time you shift your perception from separation to oneness you'll document the experience and honor the holy instant. Throughout the day, as you practice bringing love to all your relationships, you will feel a sense of peace pass over you and heighten your miracle-minded faith.

■ **Morning Reflection DAY 27**

Today's exercises will deepen your commitment to the holy instant. So let's kick it off on the right foot! Get comfortable in your meditation space and read your morning passage. Then sit in stillness and prepare for today's miracles.

Today I am a miracle worker who perceives love in everyone I see. Even my most difficult relationships are miracles. Today I am committed to bringing love to all and transcending fear through my faith in miracles. Each encounter is a holy encounter that offers me a chance to grow.

Affirmation Day 27

TODAY I AM A MIRACLE WORKER. I CHOOSE TO SEE LOVE IN ALL.

Use this affirmation whenever you encounter anyone today. Remind yourself of your true purpose and stay committed to love. Even if it's difficult—maybe you have a hard time staying committed to love when you're talking to a certain coworker or a grumpy neighbor—remain steadfast. Say to yourself, "Today I am a miracle worker. I choose to see love in all." Putting in the effort for just one day will blast open doors you thought were locked forever.

■ Evening Exercise **DAY 27**

This evening's exercise will lead you to look closely at the relationships that have caused you pain. Through the spiritual practice of witnessing these relationships with the love of your inner guide, you will be led to experience a holy instant. As it says in the *Course*, "the holiest spot on earth is one where an ancient hatred becomes a holy love." Follow the steps here and enjoy the miraculous shifts.

1. Sit in stillness for one minute and meditate on the relationships in your life. Breathe deeply in through

your nose and out through your mouth. List in your mind all the relationships in your life that cause you pain. Continue to breathe deeply in and out, allowing yourself to truly feel. Sit in this meditation for a few minutes. When you're ready, open your eyes to the room.

2. When you come out of your meditation, write in your journal the names of the people who came to mind.

3. Then say out loud to yourself: "_____ [insert person's name] is my greatest assignment. This holy encounter offers me a chance to release fear and strengthen my faith in love. I choose to see them with love." Go down the list and continue the exercise with each name in your journal.

As you lie down to sleep tonight, your exercise is to say a silent prayer for the people on your list. Remember that this week's practice creates more oneness. In your prayer, ask that these people be guided, protected, and healed from fear. Pray for them to have the same happiness you seek for yourself.

Day 28

REFLECT AND PREPARE

Today, enjoy the process of reflecting on your work from this week.

■ Morning Reflection **DAY 28**

You went big this week! Make sure to honor your process by recapping and reflecting on the work. A huge part of making this work stick is revisiting the process along the way.

■ Evening Exercise **DAY 28**

Spend time reading the introduction to Week Five. In the coming week, you'll be guided to apply these principles to your relationship to money. This will be a big week for many people, because it's imperative that you change your perception about your finances. When you raise your self-worth, you raise your net worth—and therefore support the world around you.

WEEK 5

RAISE YOUR
SELF-WORTH,
RAISE YOUR
NET WORTH

*If you dwell within abundance
you will have abundance.*

—Marianne Williamson

Each of us has our own individual relationship to money. It starts at a young age—at that time, we pick up a financial blueprint that affects us in many unique ways. Some people have grown to believe in lack and therefore never feel they have enough. Others may have grown up to believe in abundance, and as a result money flows to them freely. But regardless of our financial background, for many folks fear shows up in some way when it comes to money.

I grew up in an affluent town, but my family wasn't nearly as wealthy as those in the community, which made me feel like an outsider. Though my parents both worked hard, there was always a mentality of lack in my home. Money was a big and constant concern. As a young girl I got hooked into my parents' lack mentality, and I still struggle with that mentality in some ways today. For instance, I carry their lack with me when it comes to spending money. When I buy something new, I often feel guilty, because deep in the back of my mind linger the old memories of not having enough. I also have a hard time receiving gifts because while I was growing up I never wanted my parents to spend money they didn't have. Both these issues are related to the financial story I learned as a kid.

Though remnants of my lack-minded upbringing persist, I am proud to say that I have essentially transformed my ego's financial fear and today am abundantly minded. When I was twenty-one, I made a commitment to myself that I would never fear not having enough money. I worked to dissociate with my financial fears and instead choose abundance. This decision to transcend my lack mentality has majorly boosted my relationship to money.

Through my spiritual practice I've come to understand that when you value money as an indicator of status and self-worth, that's a sure sign your ego has intervened. The ego uses money to seek fulfillment much in the same way it uses relationships to seek fulfillment. The ego convinces you to believe that accumulating a certain amount of money can be your source of completion. Regardless of how much you have, this ego mentality supports an addictive, controlling relationship to money that will lead you to feel as though you never have enough. Each time your earning capacity hits a new level, you'll go right back to striving for more. This is a wicked cycle.

Alternatively, when you value money as a source of creating, serving, and enjoying the gifts of life, you have a much different energetic connection to your finances. When I was twenty-one, I was able to release my attachment to my family's lack, but I still closely associated money with my self-image. For instance, for years I equated my personal worth with my financial worth. This way of being was directly related to my ego's fear of financial insecurity, the fear that I'd picked up from my parents. In my case, the ego had convinced me that money equaled power and self-worth. As financial abundance came into my life, I experienced fleeting moments of excitement followed by a sense that something was missing. Why didn't these financial milestones make me feel any different? Why, after earning more, did

I still want *even more*? By the time I was twenty-nine, I experienced another quantum shift around money. As a self-reflective Spirit Junkie, I accepted the cold, hard truth: money was not the key to self-worth and happiness. My spiritual awareness helped me recognize that money, much like drugs, alcohol, sex, romance, and food, can become addictive when used as a source of happiness. I came to understand that whenever we place our happiness and peace in anything outside of ourselves, we'll inevitably feel unfulfilled and stuck. Upon accepting this, I did what any miracle worker would do: I chose a new perspective.

Through my spiritual practice I created a belief system around the value of a dollar. This work greatly served my relationship to money, as well as my earning capacity. I shifted my focus from needing money for my self-worth to wanting money to support my great work. In addition, I let go of my fear of spending and accepted that a huge part of manifesting financial abundance was to enjoy the gifts life had to offer. Finally, I consciously began to give more by donating money to charitable organizations and spiritual centers, and focusing on new ways to employ people in my business. This shift guided me to accept money as a resource to do creative, service-minded work and share more love with the world.

This week's exercises offer you an opportunity to take inventory of how you value money and create a quantum shift of your own. I'll guide you to look closely at how your ego has placed wrong-minded value on your finances. As you pay attention to your ego, you'll uncover thoughts and patterns you never knew were there. How could you? The world has placed such a huge emphasis on our earning capacity that we're all bound to get caught up in the ego's grasp. Now is your time to get out.

This week you'll move through the process of unlearning your ego's money fear. Get ready, because this work will be wildly transformational! And if you take it seriously, it will have a huge impact on your relationship to money—and your bank account.

Before we begin the week's work of undoing the ego's false perceptions, let's zero in on its tricks. To help you become the witness of your financial fears, I've outlined several ways the ego uses money as a vehicle for keeping you in the dark.

The ego blocks abundance in many ways. If you want to clear those blocks, you first have to become conscious of them. Get honest with yourself and identify whether one or more of these ego tricks has blocked your financial freedom.

- **The ego has a lack mentality.** Particularly in tough economic times, the ego will rev up its game. It busts out thoughts like *I can't possibly get a raise in a recession* or *I'll never have enough money* or *I will never afford it.* The ego has a million ways to fuel our lack mentality. The more we think in this way, the more we live in fear of not having enough. It's a dizzying circle. Remember that our thoughts inform our experiences—so know that a lack mentality mirrors a lacking bank account.

- **The ego believes that passion has no purpose when it comes to making money.** An ego mentality suggests that we must take practical action to make money. It convinces us that we can't have it both ways when it comes to earning—we can either do what we love, *or* we can make money. The ego reserves creativity and passion for hobbies, or it projects it onto the select few who get lucky enough to be financially successful with their passion work. I see this ego mentality come up a lot with my artist friends, who live in fear of never earning money from their art and, in effect, blocking any chance of doing so. I also see it in my healer friends, who believe that doing altruistic work means they'll never be well compensated. The inner dialogue of *I can't make money doing what I love* is a major ego block. I understand that this is a deep-rooted fear that affects many people, but as miracle workers we must begin to transcend this belief. When more and more people believe in abundance, more abundance will flow. We must take this very seriously and work together to create this shift.

- **The ego has a *get* mentality rather than a *give* mentality.** When we're ego minded with money, we believe we need to get more to be happy. Our peace and salvation has a dollar amount. *Giving* can often become an afterthought when *getting* is the primary function. The *Course* teaches, "To have, give all to all." This concept is confusing to the ego, but throughout your miracle-minded practice, you'll gain real clarity around the true purpose of giving.

- **The ego creates addictive patterns around money.** I've witnessed many friends struggle with money addiction, gambling addiction, and debt addiction. In many ways we can become powerless over money, which can affect every corner of our life. The belief that a certain amount of money will fix the problem is never the solution. A full-blown mental transformation is required to get out of the ego's addictive spiral.

- **The ego emphasizes the external power of money.** The power the ego gives to money is seriously damaging to us. Whenever we place power in something outside of ourselves, it's a sure sign we've aligned with the ego. If perceived wrongly, money can feel like our source of safety, security, happiness, and peace. In essence, money replaces love. When we give money this power, we're projecting one of the ego's false perceptions onto our world . . . thereby living in a constant state of needing more to feel complete. The goal of this week is to find that completeness in love and faith *instead* of money.

- **The ego uses money to deepen your belief in separation.** Money becomes a status symbol to the ego, which equates wealthy people as happy people and emphasizes the importance of external power. Because the ego thrives on separation, it uses money to further disconnect you from others. If you have money, the ego makes you more special—and if you don't, it makes you less special.

- **The ego is uncreative when it comes to money.** Ego convinces us to think in linear, limited ways—focusing on manipulative action to get more. But your *~ing* is creative and will always lead you to innovative solutions. There have been many times in my life when I wasn't sure how I would pay the bills. My ego mind never had a good solution. In fact, my ego just made the problem worse. But when I turned inward to ask my ~*ing* for help, I was always guided to a miraculous solution.

- **There's never enough for the ego.** Even if you've achieved financial abundance, the ego acts out in plenty of ways. One in particular is the "never enough" mentality. Even once the ego achieves a certain goal, it always needs more. From a spiritual perspective, when we recalibrate our faith, the Universe will provide for us. But the ego thinks quite the opposite. We're pushed to strive for more and never believe we have enough.

I'm confident that these ego projections resonate with you in multiple ways—and keep in mind they're just a few of the many ways the ego blocks your abundance. This week's work is dedicated to using subtle shifts to create powerful change in this area of your life.

Looking at how the ego has created a fearful financial blueprint can be overwhelming. In the midst of trying to pay your bills and keep your career in motion, a spiritual practice may seem like too much work. Regardless of what you have going on in your career right now, trust that it is the perfect assignment for spiritual growth. And I've got supergroovy news for you! For this week, you can take your energy off the to-do lists, the debt, and the bills. For one week, make the commitment to put your practice first and treat it like a full-time job. Go about your routine, but in your mind put this work first. Show up for the assignments with your full spirit and trust that when you awaken your internal abundance, your external abundance will be reflected. The miracle-worker practice is your full-time job. You're hired—now get to work!

Here's what you can look forward to this week:

- On **Day 29,** you will be guided to witness your financial fears. The exercises will help you identify the financial story your ego created. By acknowledging the story behind your financial fear, you'll begin the process of disassociating with it. Remember that we must witness our fear to begin the process of miraculous change.

- The work on **Day 30** will help you become willing to surrender your financial fears. This day is very powerful—a crucial step to becoming an abundant miracle worker. Each exercise will lead you to surrender to your inner guide and admit to the ways your life has become unmanageable due to your ego's fear. Honoring this unmanageability will help lead you out of any addictive patterns with money and set you up for a new financial blueprint.

- **Day 31** is geared toward a financial shift. The most effective and exciting way to kick your financial fears is to begin a new inner dialogue. The work this week will help you shift the internal and external conversation around money. If you're walking around thinking and saying you're broke, you will be broke. The exercises on Day 31 will empower you to change your inner dialogue and reclaim your financial faith and spiritual power to attract abundance.

- **Day 32** guides you to understand how gratitude creates abundance. When you're grateful for what you have, you create more of what you want. This day's exercises will guide you to focus on the abundance in your life—even the simple things such as a warm meal or $100 in your savings account. Feeling grateful for what you have helps you respect your finances.

- On **Day 33**, we work on forgiveness around your finances. Fear of finance stems from past experience, and forgiveness is the way to undo the past and start fresh in the present. The exercises on Day 33 will help you forgive your family, past employers, and yourself. You'll be guided to release the patterns through the practice of forgiveness.

- **Day 34** is dedicated to money and miracles. The exercises throughout this day will help you blast open your creative mind. You'll be guided to surrender your financial fears to your inner guide and release the blocks to your creative capacity to experience miracles.

- Then on **Day 35** you'll review the past week's exercises and prepare for the final week.

Are you committed to releasing your fears and creating a new financial blueprint? Then, my friend, this week's exercises will guide you to experience a quantum shift. This massive shift doesn't require years of practice if you're willing to surrender your fears. For the sake of your serenity and to help support our economy, we all must commit to this shift. Let the abundance set in . . .

Day 29

WITNESS YOUR
FINANCIAL FEARS

Today you're going to identify the financial story your ego created. You might already have an idea of that story—or you might be completely unaware of how your thoughts affect your finances. As you know by now, the witnessing step is crucial. You must get honest about your financial fears if you're going to change them. The only way to begin the process of disassociating from your ego is to see its falseness. Lesson 79 of *A Course in Miracles* is the reflection, "Let me recognize the problem so it can be solved." I turn to this message whenever I need a spiritual solution for the ego's perception of lack. I once spent three hours in a salon with a group of next-generation feminist writers talking about the future of feminism. During the discussion, each woman complained that she had trouble earning money as a journalist. Every member of the group reinforced the others' lack mentality, strengthening the fear around the table.

This discussion angered me. Though I had a tremendous amount of compassion for where they were coming from, I also felt a deep inner calling to "recognize the problem so it could be solved." I raised my voice and said, "There has to be a more creative way to see this." Then I went on to suggest innovative ways for journalists to earn through social media, ad sales, and strategic alliances. My disruption of the conversation brought the issue to the surface and helped the group recognize the problem. The issue was that if we focused on our lack, how could we truly lead? Highlighting the issue was the first step toward awakening to spiritual healing and creative opportunities.

This week you will do the same. You will bring your own lack mentality to the surface so that you can recognize the problem in order to solve it. By witnessing how fear has blocked your abundance, you'll open up to creative solutions. Today's practice is to recognize the problem and invite a spiritual solution.

■ Morning Reflection DAY 29

Let's begin the day with your morning reflection. Get comfortable in your meditation space. Take a deep breath in through your nose and exhale out through your mouth. Read the morning passage, and then sit in stillness for one minute. Feel all the feelings that wash over you while sitting still. Allow yourself to become aware of all the hidden emotions that live behind your financial fears.

> Today I am willing to witness my financial fears. Without judgment I pay attention to the places where I've chosen the ego. I will become conscious of how I've blocked my abundance. I know this awareness is the first right action toward reclaiming my power. When I witness my ego, I see it as

separate from who I am. This gives me the power to disassociate from my fear and realize I am not my lack mentality.

Affirmation Day 29

I AM *NOT* MY LACK MENTALITY.

Throughout the day, make an effort to be conscious of your financial fears. For instance, maybe it makes you uncomfortable to look at your bank statements. Or maybe you avoid negotiating for fear of not getting what you want. In the moment when you recognize your ego popping up, simply say: *I am not my lack mentality.* This affirmation will remind you that you've merely chosen the wrong-minded approach to money. This practice will kick off the process of disconnecting from the ego's fear.

If you're someone who often talks about lack in social settings, then you can use the acronym WAIT: Why am I talking? Each time you witness yourself engage in a lack conversation, simply say to yourself, *WAIT,* and then in your mind recite your affirmation, *I am not my lack mentality.*

Trust that by thinking or saying the words, you're creating a subtle shift that will move your focus away from fear. Remember that this path requires a moment-to-moment commitment to love. That commitment will strengthen your faith in abundance one loving thought at a time.

■ Evening Exercise **DAY 29**

The work this evening will require your pen and journal, so get cozy and crack open that notebook. Spend ten minutes ~ing-writing on the topic: *What are my financial fears and where did they come from?* Just let the pen flow and be the gentle witness to whatever fears come forward. It's important to get honest about your ego's financial perceptions in order to clear them up.

You may be very aware of where you picked up you financial fears—or maybe you didn't realize you were afraid at all. Just let your subconscious write through you and lead you to uncover the thoughts and energy that are blocking your abundance.

After your writing exercise, reread your ~ing write and say this prayer out loud:

> *Inner Guide, I am aware of my ego's financial fears. I recognize the stronghold the ego has on my life and I am willing to release it. Thank you for your guidance and support. I am not my lack mentality. I am abundant and free.*

This simple process reinforces your willingness to look at the ego and surrender your fear to your inner guide. Consciously looking at the wreckage your ego has caused is a huge part of this transformational process. Your newfound awareness of the ego's fear-based tricks will heighten your awareness of how your thoughts have sabotaged your faith in abundance. This awareness is what ignites your connection to your ~ing. Seeing your ego as separate from yourself awakens your love center and unconsciously calls on guidance. Don't be afraid to look at what the *Course* calls the ego's "tiny mad ideas." Trust that by looking, you invite love back in.

Day 30

WILLING TO CHANGE

Get ready, miracle worker, because this is going to be one powerful day. Each exercise leads you to surrender to your inner guide and admit to the ways your life has been affected by your ego's financial fear. If you're someone who has no issues with money, follow the exercises anyway. You may uncover some deep-rooted hang-ups you didn't even know were there. When you genuinely acknowledge the ways your ego's financial fears have hurt your bank account, your relationships, and your overall well-being, you'll begin to open up to change. Sometimes we have to get a little fed up with our behavior before we're ready to change it. When we admit we've hit bottom financially, then we can open up to guidance. Your willingness is the next step out of any addictive patterns with money. Now let's set you up for a new, healthy, miracle-minded financial blueprint.

■ Morning Reflection **DAY 30**

Begin the morning exercise in your meditation space. Sit up straight and take a deep breath in through your nose and exhale out through your mouth. Prepare for your morning reflection. Read it, then sit for one minute of stillness as the words settle in.

> *I recognize that my ego has projected fear onto my finances. Today I am willing to see beyond these false perceptions. I awaken my inner guidance system to lead me out of this fearful state. I am willing to change my inner dialogue about my finances. I am willing to release my fears.*

Affirmation Day 30

I AM WILLING TO CHANGE MY INNER DIALOGUE ABOUT MY FINANCES.

Today's affirmation can be layered onto your witnessing practice. As you notice your financial fears come forward, simply say out loud: "I am willing to change my inner dialogue about my finances." This statement reaffirms your willingness to see love instead of fear. Enjoy the energetic shift that this affirmation offers you. Lesson 32 of the *Course* emphasizes, "I have invented the world I see." Accepting that your internal dialogue around money has affected your external abundance will help you choose to achieve a new experience through your thoughts and words. Today's affirmation isn't pressuring you to commit to a statement you don't believe. Rather, it is opening you up to simply change the inner conversation to invent a new financial reality.

■ **Evening Exercise DAY 30**

This evening's exercise will help you deepen your awareness of the ego's tricks and heighten your willingness to see love instead. Break out your notebook and answer the following questions. Write as little or as much as you wish. Just be honest.

- In what ways do I believe in lack? For example, "I don't believe I'll ever make money in my profession." Or "I believe I'll never get out of debt."
- Do I not believe I can make money doing what I love?
- In what ways do I express a *get* mentality rather than a *give* mentality?
- Am I addicted to the high that money brings? How does that addiction show up in my life?
- Have I placed external power onto money? In what ways?
- How have my thoughts and actions reinforced my experience of lack?

Upon finishing, take a moment to reflect on what you have written. It can be tempting to judge yourself for your honest responses, but this isn't about judgment—it's about getting clear. Say this prayer for release of any judgment:

Inner Guide, once again I have taken inventory of my ego. I recognize how I have chosen wrongly and I welcome an ~ingTervention. I invite your internal guidance to come forward and lead me to transform these fears back to abundant love.

Day 31

A FINANCIAL SHIFT

Each exercise this week will help you shift your internal and external conversation around money. The most powerful way to kick your financial fears is to begin a new inner dialogue. Here's the deal: If you spend your days thinking and saying that you're broke, or poor, or struggling, you'll only strengthen your lack. Your thoughts inform your experiences—so every time you think, "I'm broke" or a similar thought, you're reinforcing *real lack*. Today's exercises require your willingness to stretch beyond your limiting beliefs and open up to a whole new perspective.

■ Morning Reflection **DAY 31**

To prepare for the powerful shifts that will take place today, let's start on solid ground. Get comfortable in your meditation space and take three deep breaths in through your nose, exhaling each out through your mouth. Then take a moment to read the morning reflection. Afterward, sit in stillness for one minute and experience the shift the words offer you.

> *Today I change my mind about my finances. I make a commitment now to focus on what I do have rather than what I lack. I pledge to consciously choose words of appreciation and abundance today.*

Affirmation Day 31

I CHOOSE TO BELIEVE IN ABUNDANCE AND ACCEPT THIS BELIEF AS MY REALITY.

Choose is the operative word in this affirmation. If you were to walk around just saying, "I believe I am abundant," it's likely that your ego would convince you not to believe it.

It's fine if you don't believe this affirmation quite yet. Changing your faith takes time. Therefore, stressing the words *I choose* will greatly help you throughout this process. Your conscious, committed decision to choose abundance over lack is all you need today. So throughout the day, when you notice your ego's lack mentality coming forward, simply say out loud, "I choose to believe in abundance and accept this belief as my reality."

As you awaken shifts in your financial perspective, you'll come to feel a sense of gratitude for your spiritual abundance. To enhance this sense of gratitude, I suggest practicing an age-old spiritual principle called tithing, which greatly adds to internal abundance. The concept of tithing suggests that you give 10 percent of your income to a place where you are spiritually fed. Possibly this donation goes to your church, temple, or even your yoga studio. At first the concept of giving 10 percent of your earnings may seem overwhelming to the ego. Let's keep it simple. This week I invite you to tithe to the best of your ability. Maybe you give 10 percent of one week's paycheck or maybe you simply write a check for $20. As a spiritual teacher I often receive PayPal-tithing checks from my Spirit Junkie followers. Whether the check is for $10 or $200, I feel the same energy of gratitude and love come through the transfer. Give as much as you feel moved to share. Giving money to a place where you're spiritually fed makes a statement to the Universe that you believe abundance must be shared. In sharing your wealth, you create more of it.

■ Evening Exercise **DAY 31**

Tonight's exercise is a feeling meditation that will help you deepen your energetic shift around your finances.

- Sit comfortably in your meditation space.

- Place your palms facing upward and take a deep breath in through your nose and exhale through your mouth.

- Think your way into a scenario where you're faced with financial fear.

- Allow all your emotions to come forward. Do not deny your feelings in any way.

- Breathe deeply into the space in your body where you feel discomfort.

- Be present in the experience of discomfort.

- As you soften into the experience of your fear gently say to yourself, *There is another way to perceive this.*

- Breathe in: *I choose to perceive abundance instead of this.*

- Breathe out: *I release my fear of finances.*

- Breathe in: *I welcome a new perspective.*

- Breathe out: *In this moment I welcome release.*

Sit in stillness for five minutes and allow your inner guide to come forward. Let the voice of love enter into your mind and lead you to new creative images. The loving voice of your *~ing* will always guide you out of fear into a new perspective.

Be patient. You may find that you have trouble accessing your *~ing* at first. This is to be expected. Always remember how powerful your ego's faith is, and don't get discouraged by its strength. *A Course in Miracles* reminds us that, "the presence of fear is a sure sign that you are trusting in your own strength." Though it may seem like a good thing to trust in your own strength, the work throughout this book is designed to help you learn to lean on a power greater than yourself. Use this meditation throughout the week and invite your inner guide to come forward for transformational healing. If even for an instant you feel relief, then a miracle has occurred. Welcome all subtle shifts.

Day 32

GRATITUDE CREATES ABUNDANCE

Good morning, miracle worker! Get psyched for today's exercises, because we're activating your gratitude muscles. By focusing on what you do have, you create energy of abundance—and that energy is what attracts more into your life. Today is all about gaining a newfound respect for your finances.

Many people who are stuck in financial fear become totally apathetic about their finances. Why? Because fear is powerful stuff—and in a misguided effort to avoid fear, they keep themselves potentially limited. Fear blocks them from looking at their bank statements, going after that awesome promotion, saving up for the stuff they love, and so on. Many folks have such a deep-rooted fear of financial instability that they avoid looking at finances altogether. This pattern creates a nasty cycle that leads to additional anxiety and discomfort.

Today's work will create subtle shifts in your behavior around your finances and offer you a new perspective for how you treat your money. It doesn't matter whether you're deep in debt or extremely wealthy: this work is important for everyone.

Mindfully respecting your finances is another way of respecting yourself. Today's work will heighten your awareness of the presence of spirit within your financial arena. New-thought writer Joseph Murphy suggests that you bless your bills and trust that God is providing for you. This is a much more grateful way of handling your finances.

■ Morning Reflection **DAY 32**

Get comfortable in your meditation space and take three deep breaths in through your nose and exhale each through your mouth. When you're ready, read the passage below. Then sit in one minute of stillness and allow your inner guide to come forward and enter into your consciousness throughout the day.

> *Today I choose to focus on all that I have. My gratitude cuts through my false belief in lack and fear. Rather than avoid my financial fears I instead focus on what I do have. I am grateful for what I have in this very moment.*

Affirmation Day 32

I AM GRATEFUL FOR WHAT I HAVE, AND I WELCOME ALL THE GIFTS THIS DAY WILL BRING.

Use this affirmation in the moments throughout the day when you get hooked into lack, fear, or self-attack around your finances. Reconnect to your abundance within when you feel without. Throughout the day, take time to affirm that you have enough in this moment.

■ **Evening Exercise DAY 32**

In the spirit of gratitude, this evening's exercise will lead you further into the practice of energetically supporting your abundance.

Make a list of all that you're grateful for. Don't leave anything out—nothing is too big or too small to make the list. Then, one item at a time, silently bless your abundance.

For example: *I am grateful for my home. I bless this abundance in my life and surround my home with love and light.*

Or another example: *I am grateful for the food on my table. I bless this meal and infuse love and light into every bite.*

Use this language and silently bless all that you are grateful for. Trust that this exercise will magnify all that is abundant in your life.

When you bring gratitude into your finances, your energy around money shifts. Gratitude leads you to honor what you do have and appreciate the simple stuff. The ego sucks you deeply in lack, comparing and attacking others and yourself. Gratitude does just the opposite. A grateful financial perspective involves loving and respecting all that you have and honors the wealth of others. The grateful miracle worker knows that the abundance you see in others is a reflection of your own capacity for abundance. Rather than get hooked into comparisons and attack, begin appreciating the abundance around you. When you honor and appreciate what you see, you become a magnet for it.

Day 33

THE "F" IN FINANCE
IS FOR FORGIVENESS

Today's exercises will further the process of undoing your false perceptions around money. Forgiveness is the catalyst for surrendering your limiting beliefs and restoring your faith in miracles. When financial fear is high, it's likely that a past belief is affecting your current behavior. Maybe you grew up with lack, and you experience lack in your life today. Or maybe you've experienced great loss of money, which makes you try to control your finances in unhealthy ways. The ego uses past financial drama in many individual ways to create chaos in the present.

This is where forgiving yourself comes in. When your self-worth is tied up in your financial worth, you're likely to have been attacking yourself for quite some time. Today, become aware of how your ego has used your finances as an attack on you. Forgiving yourself is a huge step in the process of becoming free from financial fear. Forgiving your past experiences with money will greatly benefit you, too. Through today's practice of forgiveness, you'll chip away at that false projection and establish a new perception.

■ Morning Reflection DAY 33

Let's begin this day's work with a morning reflection that will ground you in the present moment. Sit comfortably in your meditation space and take a deep breath in through your nose and exhale it through your mouth. Read the morning passage out loud and then sit in silence for one minute. Feel all the emotions that come forward from your commitment to this passage.

> *I forgive my financial history. Today I wipe away all my anger, resentment, and attack toward others and myself through the practice of forgiveness. Each choice I made in the past is exactly as it should be. Those choices guided me to this present moment. Today, forgiveness is my guide. I accept, release, and forgive my past and center back into this present moment. I let go and welcome a new experience of money.*

Affirmation Day 33

"FORGIVENESS OFFERS ME EVERYTHING I WANT."
(FROM *A COURSE IN MIRACLES*)

Today's affirmation is straight from *A Course in Miracles*. The message, "Forgiveness offers me everything I want," is the perfect reminder when it comes to releasing the ego's financial perceptions. Our ego makes us think we want a certain amount of money to make our troubles disappear, whereas what we really want is to be happy. The *Course* suggests, "Forgiveness is the key to happiness." So if you've been seeking your happiness in a certain amount of money, let's work on shifting that perspective today.

Throughout the day, use this affirmation as a reminder that you're right where you need to be. Each moment leading up to this point has offered you opportunities to learn and grow. Today is a day for true release of those past experiences so that you can embrace a new reality and feel fulfilled by your inner state of peace. Now let's fill up your love bank and throw down the F word.

■ Evening Exercise **DAY 33**

This evening's exercise leads you through a three-step financial forgiveness practice. Take your time with this exercise and know that you can return to these three steps to forgive all resentments and fears.

1. **Identify whom you need to forgive when it comes to your finances.** Maybe you need to forgive yourself for poor decisions. Maybe you need to forgive a past employer or a family member you resent. Become conscious in this moment of who is at the top of this financial forgiveness list and write his or her name down in your journal.

2. **Be conscious of your part in the situation.** Try not to overthink this step. What is your part? When you raise your awareness of how you've contributed to the difficult relationship or resentment, you can become more willing to forgive. Seeing your part in any

situation helps you detach from blame and judgment. You may even realize that the real person you need to forgive is you. For five minutes, ~ing-write on how you have contributed to any resentment.

3. **Become willing to let go of the resentment and invite your inner guide to show you what to do.** This final step is wonderful because it offers you the opportunity to release your desire to forgive and let your ~ing direct your path. As you can see by now, a major theme of A Course in Miracles is to ask the "Holy Spirit," a.k.a. ~ing, for help. When you're ready, say the following prayer out loud and call on your ~ing to lead you through the forgiveness process.

Inner Guide, I welcome you in to guide my forgiveness process. I recognize that these resentments no longer serve me and I'm ready to clear all that blocks my abundance. I surrender this relationship to you and I welcome your guidance. Show me the path to forgive.

When the three steps are complete, go to sleep knowing that you've set a powerful practice in motion. Trust that the forgiveness process is occurring without your effort. Just witness the assignments that come your way and trust the Universe has a plan. In many instances you will be given awesome opportunities to learn lessons. So if uncomfortable stuff comes up, welcome it with open arms and remember that it's an opportunity to forgive. This practice will set you free, clear your conscience, and restore your financial perceptions back to love.

Day 34

MONEY AND MIRACLES

Your ego is linear and limited, focused on to-do lists and practicality, whereas your ~ing is creative, expansive, and innovative. Today, you'll open up your creative mind—even if you don't usually think of yourself as a "creative person." Through conscious contact with your ~ing, you'll be led to heighten your awareness of miracles, thereby attracting financial abundance in ways you never could have imagined.

Miraculous support is available to us all. We just have to trust that the Universe has a plan for us and know that when we believe we're being supported, we can receive that support. *Receive* is the operative word. My coaching client Julie spent years trying to grow her business with an ego approach: overworking, controlling her hours, and pushing her limits to appease her clients. Through our work together she got into the habit of asking the Universe for help and welcoming spirit into her business. Upon accepting spirit as her business partner, she began to feel more relaxed. Her calm energy fused into her relationships with clients, her sales approach, and her overall day-to-day business. Releasing control and letting the Universe take over is exactly what Julie needed to open up her energy field to receive the business growth she'd been seeking. Like Julie, when you invite spirit into your life, you will receive more energy, guidance, and support.

■ Morning Reflection **DAY 34**

Today you're going to begin strengthening your receptivity muscles and enhancing your faith in miracles. Let's begin the day with a morning reflection on receiving. Get comfortable in your meditation space and take a few deep breaths in through your nose, exhaling each through your mouth. When you're ready, read the morning passage and then sit in stillness for one minute with your palms facing upward. This gesture suggests your willingness to receive.

> *Today I welcome infinite possibilities. With open arms I accept the support of the Universe. I know creative abundance is available to me now. I expect miracles.*

Affirmation Day 34

I WELCOME INFINITE POSSIBILITIES. I WILL RECEIVE.

Make this your mantra throughout the day. Like you did in the first weeks of your new practice, create a Miracle Moment: a calendar reminder on your computer or phone that's set up to buzz throughout the day. When you see or hear your Miracle Moment prompt, recite your affirmation. Let these words bring peace to your mind and excitement to your heart. Know that infinite creative possibilities and miracles are available to you now.

Stay committed to creative possibilities for abundance and trust in miracles. This trust takes time, so be patient and know that the more you affirm your faith, the more faithful you will be. Believing supports receiving, so take this practice seriously and amp up your faith.

■ Evening Exercise **DAY 34**

We'll close the day with a receiving meditation. You can follow the written guide here or access the audio download at gabbyb .tv/meditate.

RECEIVING MEDITATION

- Get comfortable in your meditation space.

- Sit up straight with your palms facing upward.

- Take a deep breath in through your nose, and breathe out through your mouth.

- Continue this cycle of breath throughout your meditation.

- Breathing in, invite the Universe to support and guide you.

- Breathing out, release your desires to the care of your inner guide.

- Breathe in: *I expect miracles.*

- Breathe out: *I will receive.*

- Breathe in: *I believe in creative possibilities for abundance.*

- Breathe out: *I will receive.*

- Breathe in: *I am patient and I trust.*

- Breathe out: *I will receive.*

- Breathe in: *I know I'm being guided.*

- Breathe out: *I will receive.*

Continue these mantras as you breathe in and out. Trust that you've made it clear to the Universe that you're ready, willing, and able to receive all the abundant gifts in store for you. A big part of this process is letting go of your to-do lists and controlling behavior. When you step back and settle into your miracle-minded faith, the Universe can guide you to what you need. Get out of your own way and get ready to receive!

Day 35

REFLECT AND PREPARE

t's important to understand that this week's work is just the beginning of a new financial blueprint. Your dedication to this practice will guide you toward more miraculous shifts. Money is one of the ego's greatest ways of hooking us into separation and fear. The world around you hasn't made it any easier to overcome the ego's fear. Therefore, take this week's exercises seriously and trust that the subtle shifts you've made this week have already begun a process of clearing fear and receiving abundance.

■ Morning Reflection DAY 35

As you look back on the exercises from this week, remember that true abundance stems from internal abundance. Stay committed to this truth as you continue forward in your practice. Spend time today going back over your work from this week. Take a bright pen and highlight throughout your journal the moments of breakthrough. Make a list of all the shifts that have occurred for you this week. Honor the shifts, because it is in the subtle shifts that true change occurs.

■ **Evening Exercise DAY 35**

Now it's time to prepare for the final week of this spiritual path. Take time to read the introduction to Week Six: Working Miracles. You have worked hard to shift your perceptions of yourself and your own life. Now it's time to bring this practice into your awareness of the world around you.

When you accept the invitation to become a miracle worker, you'll intuitively know that you are meant to share the love. The work in Week Six will lead you on the path toward becoming a miracle worker in the world to use your miracle mind for the highest good.

WEEK 6

WORKING
MIRACLES

If you're feeling helpless,
help someone.

—Aung San Suu Kyi

Our time spent together on this journey of new perceptions has been a daily reinforcement of the *Course* message that "only love is real." Each exercise in this book has been an invitation to your inner guide, humbly asking for guidance back to this powerful belief system. Your ~*ing* is committed to teaching you this truth as long as you continue to ask for help.

"Only love is real" is a bold statement and one that the ego cannot comprehend. This is why the *Course* doesn't suggest we deny the fear of the world but instead invite our ~*ing* to guide us to the right-minded perception of these fears. When we bring our worldly fears to our ~*ing*, we are led to find power in powerless situations—we are guided to seek solutions rather than focus on sadness. We're guided back to love. Subtle daily shifts toward love help us reposition our focus and experience miraculous perceptual shifts.

Each subtle shift you've undergone thus far has surrendered your worldly fears to your ~*ing* for healing. Each time you followed your ~*ing* instead of your ego, you invited your inner guide to reinterpret your fear from a loving perspective. In doing so, you were guided to a new perception, a miracle. Returning to your truth, you now understand that the correct, miracle-minded thing to do is not to deny your fear but rather to see fear as an assignment to learn and grow. Once you recognize this practice as a lifelong commitment, you'll realize that the transformation is not for you alone. You'll learn that you're here to use this gift to shine light on the dark world around you. You become a miracle worker in the world. As you begin to understand how love is crucial in the healing of the world, your miracle work will take on a whole new meaning. Take Gandhi, for example. Through the power of love, Gandhi moved mountains. Gandhi's faithfulness to love led India to independence and ignited movements for nonviolence, civil rights, and freedom across the world. You have the capacity to unleash your inner Gandhi and become a miracle worker in the world.

When you picked up this book, you may not have realized what you signed up for. Maybe you thought you'd heal a relationship, earn more money, or overcome an addiction. Or maybe you hoped you'd just learn to let go of some of your fear. I expect that you've begun to achieve these goals, and now it's time for you to take the next step. Being a miracle worker isn't just about letting go of negative beliefs and becoming happy: there is much, much more. Being a miracle worker is a practice of personal growth that leads to worldly transformation. The true purpose of this work is to heal your mind so you can have a greater effect on the world.

Whether you realize it or not, by picking up this book you accepted a major invitation—the invitation to help serve the world. Try not to get tripped up about this. The ego has crafty ways of keeping us from serving the world by convincing us we're helpless. As a miracle worker you now know better than to side with the ego. You now know that you're no longer powerless. The spiritual connection you have ignited is the greatest power you have to offer. The most prominent healers, teachers, and leaders are those who said no to fear and chose spirit as their guide. Miracle workers like Jesus, Buddha, Gandhi, Nelson Mandela, and Mother Teresa are powerful examples of people who chose to turn their pain into their purpose of spreading love and transformation.

These miracle-worker leaders made such huge and lasting impacts on the world because they tapped into the collective resonance. Though our ego has convinced us to perceive ourselves as separate bodies having individual experiences, the *Course* guides us to remember that there is only one of us here. We share the collective consciousness of love. Each time an individual chooses love over fear, that person becomes a bridge for all the others who choose to follow in that path. When you choose love, you create a new energetic pattern. The pattern of love becomes more accessible when more and more people choose it. The ego's world has been filled with fear, attack, judgment, and war. Now that you're on the miracle-minded path, you've chosen a new way to respond to this fear. This week we take this conscious decision more seriously, understanding the effect our choices have on the world.

A powerful example of a miracle worker whose own enlightenment greatly affected those around her was a woman named Nani Bala Barua, later called Dipa Ma. When Nani was sixteen, she married and moved to Burma with her husband. Two years later her mother died unexpectedly, leaving behind a baby boy for Nani to care for. It took Nani several years to conceive a child of her own. At the age of thirty-five, she gave birth to a daughter; only three months later her daughter died. At thirty-nine, Nani gave birth to another girl, named Dipa—which led to Nani being called Dipa Ma, or "Mother of Dipa." Following the celebration of Dipa's survival, Dipa Ma (Nani) experienced more unfortunate loss. She lost her first son during childbirth, and then, soon after, her husband died suddenly.

These losses spiraled Dipa Ma into extreme sadness and pain. She could not find solace—but rather than die from a broken heart, Dipa Ma became willing to receive help. Her willingness to surrender invited her inner guide to communicate a message in her sleep. (Often our ~*ing* will speak to us through dreams.) In her dream, Buddha appeared to give her a message: "Clinging to what is dear brings sorrow, clinging to what is dear brings fear. To one who is entirely free from endearment, there is no sorrow or fear." Dipa Ma interpreted this guidance as a sign to commit her life to Buddhism and Vipassana meditation to find true serenity and happiness. She did just that. Dipa Ma became a master in meditation.

Dipa Ma went on to teach meditation. Much like the *Course* suggests, when the teacher is ready, the students appear. Her students came in a form that reflected her: they came as household women. Dipa Ma taught women to find enlightenment in the daily practices of being a housewife. Her influence on these women led her to later be called the household saint.

Dipa Ma went on to teach some of America's most renowned Buddhist teachers, such as Joseph Goldstein, Jack Kornfield, and Sharon Salzberg. Her commitment to meditation and her faith in enlightenment influenced the world. Her spirit continues to impact spiritual seekers to this day. Dipa Ma's story reminds each of us that we have the power to effect massive change in the world, even from the comfort of our own home.

As I mentioned earlier, Dipa Ma's example reminds us that when the teacher is ready, the students will appear. This was the case for me. As soon as I committed to the *Course*, it became clear that I was to be a teacher. I started giving free talks at local women's organizations and universities. Soon I began my own lecture circuit, where I'd invite whomever I knew to attend. Audiences of forty became one hundred, then two hundred, and now exceed one thousand in person and online. The more I grew into the role of teacher, the larger my audience of students became. These students come in a form that resonates with me. Much like Dipa Ma attracted the household seekers, I've been attracting the Spirit Junkies, a new wave of spiritual seekers ready to awaken a relationship to their inner guide. As you grow your own practice, you too will be guided to teach in your own way. If you listen to your ~*ing*, you will know "where to go, what to say and what to do," as the *Course* says. Teaching love requires no level of expertise. All that is required is a desire to serve and heal.

As usual, the ego will resist miracle-minded guidance. Now that you understand how crafty the ego can be, you're well prepared to take these next steps on your path toward inner power and peace. Remember, this work requires your commitment to love and a decision to see fear differently. I offer you some powerful ways to stay connected to this week's practice.

The miracle-worker exercises throughout this week give you the groundwork for sharing your light with the world. Remember these four steps and you'll learn to follow your true calling.

One: Your purpose is to heal your mind.

Two: Continuously witness and surrender the fear that blocks your purpose.

Three: Listen to your ~*ing* and trust in the path.

Four: Choose love and know you're changing the pattern of the world.

Each day this week will awaken the miracle worker within you. The exercises throughout the book have prepared you for this week. Be the witness, stay willing, embrace the shifts, have an attitude of gratitude . . . and when in doubt, throw down an F bomb and forgive. Remember that these daily right actions are all you need to know how to serve at your highest capacity. You'll come to learn that service to the world offers you the most fulfillment and peace.

Let's start with a breakdown of the awesome exercises throughout this week that will strengthen your miracle mindset and guide you to be of service to the world.

- At this point on the path, you've raised your consciousness of how your ego can work against you. The exercises on **Day 36** help you heighten this awareness and recognize the effect your ego has on your power to serve. Each time you witness your fear throughout the day, you'll be led to remember that your purpose is to heal your mind so that you in turn can heal others through your ~*ing* guided life.
- By now you know that your willingness is crucial to living a miracle-minded life. The exercises on **Day 37** will help you surrender to the voice of your inner guide. The more willing you are, the easier it is to say yes to your inner call to serve.
- The exercises on **Day 38** shift you from a *me* mentality to a *we* mentality. This shift will come through

from the onset of the day. The repetition of this moment-to-moment decision will be a subtle shift that creates lifelong change. By continuously calling on your *~ing* for support you'll be reminded of the *we* mentality.

- **Day 39**'s work will lead you to share your gratitude with the world. You'll write a letter of gratitude to a person or organization that has greatly impacted your life. By sharing your gratitude with others, you inspire them to carry on their sacred path. Shining light on the accomplishments of others brings more light to the world.

- The practice on **Day 40** will go a long way to free you of the ego's chains. Yesterday you wrote a letter of gratitude, and today you'll write a letter of forgiveness. Putting pen to paper is one of the most powerful ways to commit to your intentions. These letters are like spiritual contracts that will support your energetic shifts. Today you'll be guided to write a forgiveness letter to a person or organization you've been unwilling to release. This letter will embody your willingness to let go of the ego's attack and awaken to a new clear mind. This clear mind is what you need to maintain constant contact with your *~ing* and be of service to the world.

- The *Course* teaches that miracle workers are students of love who have committed to sharing their positive perceptions with the world. Accepting your own healing is the first step toward becoming a miracle worker. The next step is to share that love through your thoughts, energy, and actions. The exercises on **Day 41** will help you accept the next phase in your spiritual development, which is to carry the message of love.

- For the last day of this process, **Day 42**, I will guide you to reflect on and honor your work and spiritual growth. You will throw a miracle party and invite one or more friends to join you in celebration of you!

So let's get the love parade moving and take the next right action toward becoming a miracle worker in the world. As you deepen your practice this week, ask yourself, *What am I choosing to bring to the world?* Do not judge your past; rather, honor the path you've taken and accept that it's been your learning device to get to where you are. Know today that you are not alone—and as we go through this life together, we have the choice to bring more love or pollute the world with more fear. Today, choose love.

Day 36

WITNESS YOUR WAYS IN THE WORLD

Your work thus far has prepared you to understand how your ego works. By now you know when your ego has you in a headlock—and today's exercises are geared toward heightening this awareness and recognizing the ways your ego can affect your capacity to serve others. Each time you witness your fear throughout the day, you'll detach from the ego's stronghold. Each time you dissociate from the ego, you're led to remember that your purpose is to heal your mind so you can help others.

A *Course in Miracles* says: "Miracles are healing because they supply a lack; they are performed by those who temporarily have more for those who temporarily have less." This passage reinforces the role of the miracle worker in the world. As you heal your mind and help others shift their fears to love, you perform a miracle. What the *Course* means by those who "temporarily have more" is that those people are in their right minds, sharing love with people in their wrong minds who "temporarily have less." The goal of today's work is to begin the practice of witnessing when you temporarily have more and how you can serve to heal the wrong-minded fear of others. When you heal your mind, you invite the healing of others to occur. Therefore, today's work is to witness your fear for your sake and for the service of the world.

■ Morning Reflection DAY 36

The morning reflection today will greatly serve your loving perceptions. Prepare your meditation space for five minutes of self-reflection. When you're comfortable, read the morning passage that follows and sit for one minute of stillness. Following your stillness, write down in your journal whatever comes to mind. Let your inner guide come forward the moment you awaken from your contemplative state.

> *Today I witness my ego in action. I patiently look upon my false perceptions with loving lenses. I no longer believe in this fear. I am no longer attached to this fear. Though it may seem real in the moment, all I have to do is witness it without judgment to be reminded it is not true.*

Affirmation Day 36

FOR MY PEACE AND THE PEACE OF THE WORLD, I CHOOSE LOVE.

The ego probably will be uncomfortable with this affirmation because the ego's faith in fear is very strong. When you affirm statements like this, you may experience a sense of conflict and confusion. This is to be expected, so allow the confusion to occur, knowing that it's part of the process. Stay committed to your true purpose, which is to heal your wrong-minded perceptions so you can bring more light to the world. Throughout the day recite the affirmation to yourself: *For the sake of my peace and the peace of the world, I choose love.*

Let these words take on a life of their own. Much of the miracle-worker practice is about allowing the energy behind the affirmations to guide our energy to shift accordingly. Trust that by simply reciting this affirmation throughout the day you're recalibrating your own energy and therefore shifting the energy patterns of the world.

■ **Evening Exercise DAY 36**

This evening, before you go to sleep, I will lead you in a loving-kindness meditation. This meditation sets the stage for the week ahead and primes you with the energy of service and surrender. This meditation kicks off your week with all the power energy you need to amplify your practice and surrender to your role as a miracle worker in the world. You can either follow the meditation here or listen to my guided meditation at www.gabbyb .tv/meditate.

LOVING-KINDNESS MEDITATION

- Get comfortable in your meditation space.
- Sit up straight in your seat.
- Take a deep breath in through your nose and exhale it through your mouth.

- Continue this cycle of breath throughout your meditation.

- Hold an image in your mind of a beautiful ball of light in your heart.

- See this light extend from your heart into every corner of your life.

- Envision the light extending into your home . . .

- Into your workplace . . .

- Into your local community.

- As you breathe in and out, see the light extend from your heart to other areas of the world.

- Breathe in love.

- Breathe out kindness to the world.

- With each inhale and exhale, you extend light, love, and kindness to the world around you.

- Soon all you see is light.

Day 37

LISTEN UP!

Now that you've called on your *~ing* for help, it's time to say YES to the call. The exercises today will help you embrace the voice of love. The more open you are to receiving guidance, the easier it will be to say yes to the inner call for love and service.

Saying yes often is crucial to your practice. The ego will do everything in its power to keep you from listening to the voice of love. As your practice grows, you can trust that the ego will work harder. Therefore, it is imperative to soften the ego's conviction with the power of love. Once again, be mindful of the ego's sneaky ways and wholeheartedly surrender to say yes to your inner voice of love.

■ Morning Reflection DAY 37

Begin the day with a surrender prayer. Offer up your plans to the care of your inner guide and state your willingness to listen.

Get comfortable in your meditation space and place your palms facing upward—this position is a reminder to the Universe that you're willing to receive guidance. Take a deep breath in through your nose and exhale through your mouth. When you're ready, read the morning reflection and then sit for one minute of stillness.

> *Today I surrender my plans, my will, and my fears to the care of my inner guide. I accept that there is a greater plan for me than what my small mind may have had in store. Today I welcome the voice of love to come forward and guide me, teach me, and lead me to a happier state of mind so I can bring more light to the world.*

Affirmation Day 37

INNER GUIDE, I WELCOME YOU TO SHOW ME WHERE TO GO, WHAT TO DO, AND WHAT TO SAY.

State this affirmation throughout the day. Make it your mantra (a single pointed thought). When you reaffirm the desire to receive guidance, you will be amazed by the guidance you receive.

■ Evening Exercise **DAY 37**

Tonight is an exercise in saying yes to your ~*ing's* call for love. Let the spirit of your inner guide move through you.

Make a list of all the issues that have been troubling you—whether it be a fear of not having enough money, fear that you cannot leave a relationship, or fear of not living out your life's purpose. Simply get honest about what fears are present in you today. It's likely that these fears have less of a hold on you than they did in your first week of this practice. It's also possible that new, deeper emotions may be coming forward due to your commitment to grow. This exercise helps you surrender once again to your inner guide and activate an even greater connection to love.

Look closely at the list and invite your ~*ing* in for healing. Read what you've written, then recite the following prayer out loud. Go one by one down the list and recite this prayer for each fear on your list.

> *Inner Guide, I turn my fears over to you. I know that I have a greater purpose than to dwell in fear. Please take this from me now.*

Then sit in stillness and let inspiration flow through you. Trust that your ~*ing* will have no trouble calling on creative, loving thoughts to shine love into your darkest corners.

This exercise helps you to see your fear head-on and choose love instead. You are ready now to do this, and it's a crucial part of the practice. This work will clear your energy so you can shine brighter in the world. Embracing your spiritual connection is like being given a supercharged power outlet that you can always plug into. Knowing this outlet is available at any time will give you the strength to serve and the faith you need to live in love and be of high service. Take this seriously and you will experience a tremendous sense of relief. Repositioning your fear through your connection to your ~ing is a practice I hope you'll use forever.

Day 38

SHIFT FROM *ME* TO *WE*

Five years ago I experienced a miraculous shift from a *me* mentality to a *we* mentality. At the time I was lecturing throughout the country and receiving a lot of e-mail requests from women for help. My ego loved that others needed me. I would stay up all night responding to e-mails, only to wake up the next day totally depleted. My ego convinced me to believe that because I was helping everyone else, I was good enough. I came to realize that this codependent pattern of overly serving everyone was not serving me or the world. My need to feel needed was a *me*-based approach to love.

This behavior didn't sit well with me. Deep down I knew there had to be a better approach to serving these women. I sat in meditation and listened to my inner guide. My intuition spoke loud and clear and said, "Get online and serve through the Internet!" My *~ing* was leading me to use the resources on the Internet to serve more people with the same intention. I was led to create the social networking site HerFuture.com for women to gather on the Internet to inspire, empower, and connect with one another. This guidance was leading me to let the collective *we* take over and stop thinking that I was the only one who could help. The site became a space where all kinds of incredible women could come together to serve one another. By shifting my focus from a *me* mentality to a *we* mentality, I was able to create a home for thousands of women to share and serve. This *we* approach was the greatest gift I could offer the world.

The exercises today will help you shift from a *me* mentality to a *we* mentality. Each exercise is designed to awaken your subconscious to open up to new ways of spreading love. The ego wants us to believe that alone we can save the world. Our individual work is important, but an honest approach to service requires faith in the collective *we*.

Your morning reflection will launch this shift, and repeating this moment-to-moment decision will propel it throughout the day. By continuously calling on your *~ing* for support you'll be reminded of the *we* mentality.

■ Morning Reflection **DAY 38**

Let's begin today's shifts with a powerful morning reflection. Get situated in your meditation space and read the following passage to yourself. Then sit in stillness for one minute and allow your *~ing* to come forward and guide the shifting process.

> *Today I prepare to shift my focus from a me mentality to a*
> *we mentality. When I am of service to others, I get out of my*
> *own way and stop focusing on my own inner turmoil. Today*

I choose to shift my attention from my internal dialogue by consciously paying attention to others. I will listen to those who want to be heard. I will help those who are in need. I will guide those who are lost. I will serve those who call for love.

Affirmation Day 38

I WILL LISTEN TO THOSE WHO WANT TO BE HEARD, HELP THOSE WHO ARE IN NEED, GUIDE THOSE WHO ARE LOST, AND SERVE THOSE WHO CALL FOR LOVE.

Write this affirmation on a piece of paper and put it in your pocket. Throughout the day, whenever you notice your ego come up, take the affirmation out of your pocket and recite it to yourself. Let this affirmation guide you to shift your *me* thoughts to *we* thoughts in an instant. Refocus your attention each time you reach into your pocket for guidance.

■ Evening Exercise **DAY 38**

This evening's exercise is more action oriented than usual. Tonight you are going to step outside your comfort zone and do something kind for someone else. The action you take this evening will be uncomfortable for your ego. The ego has a strong need to focus on serving yourself first, for fear that there won't be enough love to go around. The *Course* teaches the exact opposite mentality: that when we serve others, we greatly serve ourselves. Tonight you will experience the miracle of what true altruism can bring.

Take a moment to think of someone in need. It can be someone you know directly or someone you don't know at all.

Next, read the Saint Francis prayer that follows here. (Throughout my spiritual journey I've often turned to this prayer for a powerful reminder to shift into a *we* mentality.) After reading the prayer, sit in stillness briefly, then allow the accompanying service meditation to guide you. Following the meditation, sit quietly again to listen to your inner guide and take loving action toward being of service to someone else.

The Saint Francis prayer is one of the greatest messages for service and interconnectedness. Enjoy.

PRAYER OF SAINT FRANCIS

Lord, make me an instrument of your peace.
Where there is hatred, let me sow love.
Where there is injury, pardon.
Where there is doubt, faith.
Where there is despair, hope.
Where there is darkness, light.
Where there is sadness, joy.
Grant that I may not so much seek to be consoled, as to
    console;
to be understood, as to understand;
to be loved, as to love.
For it is in giving that we receive.
It is in pardoning that we are pardoned,
and it is in dying that we are born to Eternal Life.
Amen.

SERVICE MEDITATION

- Sit comfortably in your meditation space.

- Breathe deeply in through your nose and out through your mouth.

- Continue this cycle of breathing throughout the meditation.

- Invite your inner guide to enter into your meditation.

- Say in your mind: Inner Guide, help me get out of my own way. Help me be of service to someone else. Please show me who to serve and how to serve. What miracles would you have me perform?

- Sit in stillness and listen to your inner guidance system.

After a few minutes of sitting in stillness, write down the direction you received from your inner guide. If you don't experience a strong sense of direction right away, trust that it is coming. You will be guided to know how to serve. If you do experience this direction quickly, then take action immediately. This service action can be as simple as calling someone to see if they need help, washing your roommate's dishes, or dialing the number to donate money to a charitable organization. Trust the voice of love that is guiding you and commit fully to serve.

It is important that you commit to this action as soon as you get the hit to be of service. Any delay will open the door for your ego to get in the way with excuses and personal distractions. Try your best to follow your inner guidance to be of service.

Once you have taken action, trust that you have done the right thing. Your ego will always interfere and try to convince you that you've gone too far, spent too much, or wasted your time. Instead of succumbing to the ego, sit in stillness and enjoy the beautiful benefits of your service.

Day 39

GRATITUDE TO THE WORLD

The exercises today will lead you to share your gratitude with the world and will help you let the world off the hook. The simple truth is that you can't expect the outside world to make you happy. Happiness is an internal condition that doesn't require outside influence. When you stop trying to make the world serve you, then *you* can serve the world.

Gratitude guides this process. The ungrateful ego is the faultfinder; it will always look for problems. Once again, today, you'll strengthen your gratitude muscles and release the ego's false projections.

■ Morning Reflection **DAY 39**

Get comfortable in your meditation space. Read the reflection passage slowly, letting each word settle in. Then sit for one minute of stillness as your *~ing* comes forward to soak up the words and lead the way.

*Today I am grateful for the world around me. I am grateful
for the lessons I've learned and the new growth opportunities
ahead. I am grateful for my new loving perceptions of the
world.*

Affirmation Day 39

I AM GRATEFUL FOR MY NEW PERCEPTIONS OF THE WORLD.

Today's affirmation brings gratitude to the world you've projected. Acknowledging your new vision of the world is important to your miracle-worker practice. As you know by now the ego will resist your loving perceptions at all cost. Therefore, it's important to celebrate your new perspective by practicing today's affirmation. Remember that the *Course* teaches that projection is perception. What you project internally you will perceive externally. When you project an inner state of gratitude, you bring light to your external perceptions. Each time you affirm your loving perspective of the world you dissociate from fear and flat out feel better. Your loving feelings will be felt by everyone around you as they vibrate throughout the atmosphere. Use this affirmation throughout the day to guide your internal projections and energy back to love.

■ Evening Exercise **DAY 39**

This evening, your exercise is to write a letter of gratitude to a person or organization that has greatly affected your life. This practice is guaranteed to bring you happiness—but it also will have a wonderful effect on the other people involved. By sharing your gratitude with others, you inspire them to carry on their sacred path. Shining light on the accomplishments of others brings more light to the world.

There is no right or wrong way to write this letter. Simply write from your heart. Share all that you are grateful for and pour your truth onto the page. The goal is to feel the experience of gratitude come forth as you openly share your appreciation. The energy of gratitude that is ignited within you will be felt throughout the ether. If you feel moved to share the letter, feel free to press Send on an e-mail or stamp an envelope. If you don't feel moved to share it, you can trust that the energy of the message is being picked up no matter how far away the other party may be. The energy of gratitude is pure love and can penetrate all time and space. Extend your love and light to the world with this beautiful gift of gratitude.

Day 40

A LETTER OF FORGIVENESS

Today's practice is a huge step toward disconnecting from the ego's hold. Each exercise today helps to clear the inner attack thoughts that have held you back from serenity. This clear, serene mind is what you need to maintain constant contact with your ~ing and be of service to the world.

Forgiveness is the greatest gift you have to offer the world. The bold commitment to forgive your ego's falseness is the true catalyst for miracles. If you are ready to be a miracle worker in the world, then the F word must be your mantra.

■ **Morning Reflection DAY 40**

Get comfortable in your meditation space and prepare for today's morning reflection. This morning you are going to take a bold step forward toward forgiving your ego's false projections. Read the passage and sit for one minute in stillness, allowing the magnitude of the intention to set in.

I forgive the false projections I have placed on the world. I forgive myself for choosing these attack thoughts, and I forgive all those involved in the fear I have created. Through forgiveness I set myself free from the fearful world I projected.

Day 40 Affirmation

I FORGIVE THE FALSE PROJECTIONS I HAVE PLACED ON THE WORLD.

As it says in Lesson 75 of the *Course* workbook: "Today we celebrate the happy ending to your long dream of disaster. The light has come. I have forgiven the world." Through forgiveness you can end your illusion of fear. Today's affirmation changes your mind about your fear of the world. Each time you forgive your fear you acknowledge it is false. When you believe in fear, the world you see is fearful. By forgiving the false projections you have placed on the world, you can disconnect from the ego's stories, images, and attack. You can be set free from the fear of the world and choose to see love instead.

Throughout the day, when you notice a fearful projection placed on your worldly experience, simply say to yourself: *I forgive the false projections I have placed on the world.* Even the most mundane circumstances, like getting impatient with a bank teller or thinking a negative thought about a stranger, can be an attack on the world. In these moments, regardless of how insignificant they may seem, I encourage you to say your affirmation. Each thought you have either supports the positive energy of the world or pollutes it. Be mindful of your thoughts.

■ Evening Exercise DAY 40

This evening we're going to rock the F word once again. Your exercise is to write a forgiveness letter to a person or organization you've been resenting. I don't expect you to share it (unless you choose to do so). Instead, use this process as an opportunity to clean house. This letter will embody your willingness to banish the ego's attack and awaken to a new clear mind.

Get clear about a person or organization you've been resenting greatly. Maybe you're holding on to anger toward a past employer. Or maybe you're resentful of your opposing political party. Holding on to these resentments won't serve you or the world. Get honest with yourself about the ways your resentment has been holding you back from stepping into your true service. How has your ego held you back from forgiving? In what ways has this resentment negatively affected your life? How has this resentment held you back from living in your power and sharing your light with the world? Let your realization of the ego's negative impacts become the impetus for you to go ahead and surrender to writing the letter. There is no right or wrong way to write this letter. All that matters is that your intention is clean. With clear purpose release your resentment onto the page and wrap it with love and forgiveness.

When you're finished writing the letter, bring it to your meditation space for a ritual. Read the letter to yourself and ask your inner guide to show you how to forgive. Recite the following prayer from *A Course in Miracles*:

> To everyone I offer quietness.
> To everyone I offer peace of mind.
> To everyone I offer gentleness.

Day 41

YOU ARE A MIRACLE WORKER

Today, remember that your impact on the greater consciousness is directly related to the choice you make in this moment. Take your choice for love very seriously. Today, when you choose love, you bring more love to the world. The *Course* teaches that miracles are habits that should be involuntary. As you deepen your miracle-minded path, your choice for love becomes natural and miracles extend from you each time you make the right-minded decision to surrender your fear. Today's practice opens you up to accept your role as a miracle worker who is committed to choosing love in all dark situations. Each choice for love supplies lack with light and offers the world a blessing.

■ **Morning Reflection DAY 41**

Let's begin your morning reflection by igniting miracles through a powerful prayer from *A Course in Miracles*.

PRAYER FROM *A COURSE IN MIRACLES*
[YOU CAN REPLACE "HIM" AND "HE"
WITH "MY *INNER GUIDE*"]

I am here to be truly helpful.
I am here to represent Him who sent me.
I do not have to worry about what to say or what to do,
because He who sent me will direct me.
I will be healed as I let Him teach me to heal.

Allow this prayer to create a direct line of communication between your ~ing and your right mind. Trust that this prayer has kicked off your day in the most powerful direction. Now your job is to surrender and listen for the guidance.

Affirmation Day 41

§ I AM HERE TO BE TRULY HELPFUL.

I love to make this my mantra! As a committed miracle worker, this line from *A Course in Miracles* is my go-to affirmation whenever I notice my ego sneak in. (You can only imagine how often I use this affirmation.) Regardless of how far we come on our miracle-minded path, the ego will always find ways to rain all over the love parade.

Having this affirmation in your back pocket is like having a fire extinguisher for the ego. I encourage you to include this affirmation in your daily practice from this point forward. Whenever you notice your ego fire up, snuff out the flames by affirming: *I am here to be truly helpful.*

Each time we reiterate our desire to be of service, we get out of our own way and remember our true purpose.

■ **Evening Exercise DAY 41**

This evening's exercise is about . . . having more fun! On the eve of 2012, I announced that my New Year's resolution was to measure my success by how much fun I'm having. Though this intention has greatly benefited me individually, it has also had a major impact on the world. When I made fun my primary intention, the energy of love began to bleed through everything I did. Love came through each meal I made, each tweet I tweeted, and every talk I shared. Love extended from me as a gift to the world.

When you make fun your primary purpose, you will experience many miracles and be of high service to the world. So tonight's exercise is to become aware of all the ways you can ignite more fun.

Let's revisit the areas of your life we addressed in this course. Touching on each area of your life, identify where you can inject more straight-up fun. In your journal, respond to the following questions:

- **The Self Lover:** In what ways can I have more fun on my own and in everyday life?
- **The Miracle of the Body:** How can I enjoy the process of physical activity? What innovative and challenging workouts can I try? How can I enjoy the process of eating healthful foods?
- **Holy Relationships:** How can I bring more fun into my relationships? What thoughts, conversations, ac-

tions, and activities can I incorporate into all my relationships?

- **The Miracle of Abundance:** How can I bring more
  fun into my career or place of work? How can I have
  fun while I'm creating abundance?
- **The Miracle Worker of the World:** How can I bring
  more fun to the world?

The next part of this exercise offers you guidance to continue your miracle-worker practice far beyond this six-week pro-
gram. For the next month I encourage you to exercise *fun* at
least once in each of these areas of your life.

Throw a party for yourself to celebrate your hard work.
Cook a beautiful meal and enjoy sharing it with others. Test-
drive a cool, out-of-the-ordinary workout (check out the many
suggestions I included in my first book, *Add More ~ing to Your
Life*). Experience a fun adventure with another person. Get together with your coworkers socially and deepen your connections. Smile more as you travel throughout your life.

The most significant point of this exercise is to raise your
overall love energy. When you raise your love energy, you bring
more love to the world. The experience of love is the greatest
gift you have to offer—because love breeds more love.

These are among many simple examples of igniting more
fun in your world. Remember, as Wayne Dyer says, your intentions create your reality. When you intend to have fun, you
have a fun life. Simple as that.

Day 42

REFLECT AND CELEBRATE

Today is the last day of the miracle-worker journey . . . so let's go out with a bang! You'll begin this day with a powerful morning prayer from *A Course in Miracles*.

■ Morning Reflection **DAY 42**

As always, get comfortable in your meditation space and take a few deep breaths in through your nose and exhale through your mouth. When you're ready, read the Morning Prayer out loud.

A COURSE IN MIRACLES MORNING PRAYER

How lovely is the morning! All the things
Of earth are fresh and newly born again.
The ravages that seemed to wear away
The newness in which yesterday began
Have been restored. The world's recovery

Shines on each blade of grass and every leaf
That sings again of morning. And God's Voice
Calls to His Son to make another choice.

This is a day of celebration, a time to reflect on the incredible work you've done. Follow the guided meditation here, or listen to my guided meditation at www.gabbyb.tv/meditate.

After the meditation, do an ~*ing* write in which you share your experience of your new miracle-worker practice. Let it all out. Document your excitement for the powerful work you have done. Honor yourself through each and every word.

CELEBRATION MEDITATION

- Get comfortable in your meditation space.

- Sit up straight with your palms facing upward.

- Take a deep breath in through your nose and breathe out through your mouth.

- Continue this cycle of breath throughout your meditation.

- Breathe in: *Today I celebrate myself!*

- Breathe out: *Today I am proud of the steps I have taken.*

- Breathe in: *Today I accept my role as a miracle worker in the world.*

- Breathe out: *Today I surrender to my true purpose.*

- Breathe in: *I am love.*

- Breathe out: *I share love.*

- Breathe in: *I am love.*

- Breathe out: *I share love.*

- Breathe in: *I am love.*

- Breathe out: *I share love.*

- Close your meditation by breathing in a huge sigh of relief knowing you have begun a transformational journey of new perceptions. You are a miracle worker in the world!

Following this meditation, take some time for stillness. Allow yourself to surrender to the loving spirit energy that surrounds you. Soak it up and revel in the love. Enjoy this beautiful day. Be proud of how far you've come. Know that with this practice, anything is possible.

Know you are love.

Though we are done with the forty-two-day plan, the real work has just begun. Living the miracle-worker way requires true commitment. In the final chapter, I'll hook you up with clear guidelines for strengthening your connection to your *~ing* and staying on course as a full-on miracle worker.

> *Love cannot exist as a monologue; it is a dialogue, a very harmonious dialogue.*
>
> —OSHO

Conclusion

LIVING A MIRACULOUS LIFE

Without your smile, the world cannot be saved.

—*A COURSE IN MIRACLES*

In 1957, a group of Tibetan monks was informed that they would have to move their sacred shrine because a highway was being built on that land. A focal point of their inhabitance was a huge clay Buddha, which also had to be relocated. Moving the Buddha was no small feat. The monks arranged to have a crane move the Buddha to their new location. The moment they started lifting the Buddha on the crane, the clay began to crack. To make matters worse, rain was pattering down, deepening and widening the cracks. To protect the Buddha from further damage after it had been moved, the monks covered it with tarps overnight. During the evening, the head monk went under the tarps with a flashlight to check on the clay Buddha. Upon shining light on the Buddha the monk noticed golden shimmers of light radiating from the cracks. He brought back his chisel and hammer to chip away at the clay and uncover the shimmer from within the Buddha's frame. As the monk chipped away at the clay Buddha, he realized that it was not clay after all—the Buddha was made of gold.

Surprised by this discovery, the monks were eager to determine the heritage of this Buddha. They learned that many centuries earlier, their predecessors worshiped the Buddha in its golden form. These ancestral monks got word that the Burmese army was coming to destroy their community and attack them, so they covered the Buddha with clay to protect it. The monks were killed in the attack, but the army placed no value on the clay Buddha and therefore left it unharmed.

I decided to conclude this book with the story of the Golden Buddha because it offers us all a beautiful metaphor for our own lives. Inside we're all Golden Buddhas, but we grew to believe we were made of clay. Our ego's false perceptions led us to grow into a belief system that covered our inner light. We've spent years, maybe decades, masking our truth. Now it's time to embrace our light and reconnect with our Golden Buddha within.

The work you've undergone in the past six weeks has embodied the symbols of the flashlight, the chisel, and the hammer. Each week your flashlight shined upon your dark mind with the willingness to look at the ego's illusions. Then with your chisel you began to chip away at your clay exterior by shifting your perspective, practicing gratitude, and embracing forgiveness. And with your hammer you've broken through layers of darkness to unleash your golden inner light, uncovering many miracles in the process.

Day 42 is complete, but your journey has just begun. The

path we've walked together merely chipped away at the clay cov-
ering your gold. Now your job is to keep chiseling to uncover
more and more love each day.

Be mindful that the ego will do everything in its power to
sabotage your practice. Typically, one of two things happens at
this point in the process:

1. You become so inspired by the work that you commit
   to these principles in all your affairs, deepening your
   spiritual practice more and more each day.
2. You feel great and therefore conclude that the work is
   over. Within a few weeks (maybe even days), the ego
   convinces you that you're healed and no longer need
   the daily practice. You lose sight of your miracle mind-
   set.

I bring up these potential scenarios to raise your awareness
of what happens when the ego sabotages the commitment
you've made. Remember that your ego has been with you a
lifetime—whereas you just kicked off your practice six weeks
ago. Therefore, it's your job to stay committed to choosing your
~ing over your ego and embracing your Golden Buddha within.

A Course in Miracles asks us if we'd rather be host to love or
hostage to the ego. Each new day offers you the opportunity to
decide for love, inviting your ~ing as your teacher, or to succumb to the ego's false guidance. Your happiness is determined
by the moment-to-moment decision to choose love over fear.

If you choose the first option and stay committed to the
miracle-minded way, you will know a new peace and happiness.
You'll rightly perceive obstacles as opportunities, and you will

instinctively know how to navigate through whatever life brings. When you live with a miracle mind-set, you wake up each day knowing that the world is your classroom and people are your assignments. If you continue the principles taught in this practice, you will surrender these assignments to the care of your inner guide and patiently stick around for the miracles.

This closing chapter's purpose is to inspire you to deepen your commitment to miracles so that you don't let the ego sabotage your happiness. Remember: this work is about progress, not perfection. All I hope for you is that you do your best to choose your miracle mind-set as often as possible. When the ego creeps in (which it always will), your job is to consciously return to love.

Outlined below is a recap of the seven daily principles from this practice. If you make these principles a sacred part of your daily right actions, you will be hooked up with love and have a heightened awareness of the ego. Remember that our goal isn't to kill the ego; rather, our goal is to become so aware of the ego that we no longer give it power.

The Principles

By now you're well accustomed to the seven principles to move us closer to love, which you can practice every day:

- Be the gentle witness.
- Be willing to choose love.
- Shift your perspective.
- Foster a gratitude attitude.
- Practice the F word.

- Expect miracles.
- Reflect and recap.

These principles will be your guide each week as you move forward in your practice. I've separated these principles into three sections: the **flashlight**, the **chisel**, and the **hammer**. Much like the story of the Golden Buddha, you too need these tools to uncover your light. With your flashlight you shine light on the ego's darkness. With your chisel you awaken to a miracle mind-set. And with your hammer you crack open to awaken your spiritual connection. Your job isn't to figure everything out, but rather invite your inner guide to be your teacher. In time, the principles will become second nature and you will use them interchangeably. At any given moment you will be able to reach into your spiritual toolbox and clean up the ego's nasty tricks. Here's how it all comes together.

THE FLASHLIGHT

Your witnessing practice, your willingness to change, and your miraculous shift in perception are the flashlight that will help to awaken from the darkness of the ego. Use these three steps throughout each day to help light the way of your path.

The *Course* suggests: "Do not be concerned about how you can learn a lesson so completely different from everything that you have taught yourself. How would you know? Your part is very simple. You need only recognize that everything you learned you do not want. Ask to be taught and do not use your experiences to confirm what you have learned." This message is crucial to using your flashlight principles properly. Accept that your job isn't to make things right, but instead to fearlessly shine light on what is wrong and let your inner guide lead you to learn and grow.

Be the Gentle Witness

Remember the key principle of the witnessing process is to be nonjudgmental. The *Course* teaches not to judge your ego with your ego. There is no right or wrong way to do this work. Your job is just to witness your ego in action and consciously remind yourself of the false perceptions you have chosen. Throughout your witnessing process it will be powerful to call on the *Course* affirmation: "I am not the victim of the world I see." Each moment you witness the dark illusions of your ego, call on this affirmation for serenity and clarity.

As you deepen your practice of witnessing, you'll come to accept the *Course*'s message that "there are no idle thoughts." It will become easier and easier to identify how your fearful thoughts block you from your truth. In time you'll come to accept what the *Course* teaches: "Peace of mind is clearly an internal matter. It must begin with your own thoughts, and then extend outward." As you witness your own thoughts you'll begin to have the willingness to change them.

Be Willing to Choose Love

Each moment we can be the host to love or the hostage to the ego. Have the willingness to let go of yesterday and see today as new. Choosing your ~-ing as your guide is a moment-to-moment decision that only requires your *willingness* to decide for love.

Heighten your willingness by staying connected to the *Course* affirmation, "I choose to see love instead of this."

Each instant you become aware of your distress, simply use this *Course* reminder: "There is another way of looking at the world." Remember that your ego will work hard to keep you from awakening the willingness to choose your ~*ing*. With this knowledge, consciously stay alert to the ego's tricks and remember what the *Course* teaches: "The ego analyzes; the Holy Spirit accepts." Each time you become willing to choose your ~*ing* over your ego, you release your self-made teacher and surrender to your inner guide.

Shift Your Perspective

The final element of the flashlight is your miraculous shifts in perception. The *Course* teaches: "The truth is that you are responsible for what you think, because it is only at this level that you can exercise choice." Every thought you have makes up some segment of the world you see. Therefore, you must work with your thoughts if your perception of the world is to be changed. By witnessing your fear and being willing to see love, you prepare yourself for the shift. When you shift your perspective, the miracle occurs. Every situation, properly perceived, becomes an opportunity to heal.

THE CHISEL

Positioning a chisel to crack something open takes a lot of intention. Your flashlight has awakened your willingness to change, and with your chisel the process sets in. As you become more aware, your focus on gratitude and forgiveness becomes more present. The chisel represents these qualities of the miracle worker.

Foster a Gratitude Attitude

Each new day, intend to be grateful. The simple desire for gratitude unlocks your heart to receive the gifts of love around you. If even for one moment you place gratitude before your ego's fear, you will create the holy instant. Allow gratitude to be your guide to new perceptions and strengthen your willingness to forgive.

Practice the F Word

The *Course* teaches, "The light of the world brings peace to every mind through my forgiveness." Place much attention and focus on the F word. Your quantum shifts will come through forgiveness. The *Course* guides us to understand that "forgiveness means 'to give forth.' To give forth everything. To not hold on to anything. To let go of fear, guilt and pain." Each day, commit to choosing happiness over the ego's need to be right. Forgiveness is the key to your happy relief.

Forgiveness is something we allow. Remain willing to forgive and allow your inner guide to lead the way. All that is required is your willingness. Enjoy the happy gifts forgiveness offers you. *A Course in Miracles* says, "In kind forgiveness will the world sparkle and shine, and everything you once thought sinful now will be reinterpreted as part of Heaven. How beautiful it is to walk, clean and redeemed and happy, through a world in bitter need of the redemption that your innocence bestows upon it! What can you value more than this? For here is your salvation and your freedom. And it must be complete if you would recognize it."

THE HAMMER

The final two principles represent the hammer that will crack you open to your own inner light. Living a miraculous life requires faith and commitment to miracles. Expecting miracles is the part of the process that helps all the other principles set in. Without faith in miracles, your work cannot stick. If you are ready to live a life dedicated to love, then miracles must be an expectation, not a distant afterthought.

Expect Miracles

This work does not require major heavy lifting, especially in the final principles. A *Course in Miracles* says, "The miracle comes quietly into the mind that stops an instant and is still." Your stillness is required for true shifts to occur. I find for myself that I can practice witnessing, willingness, gratitude, and forgiveness—but without deep stillness I cannot let the miracle set in.

My message for you is to slow down so you can experience the miracle. Through your meditation practice and conscious decisions to shut off the computer or phone, you can find moments of stillness that will offer up the most miraculous guidance. A moment is all you need.

Miracles extend far beyond your personal experience. The *Course* teaches, "A miracle is a service. It is the maximal service you can render to another. It is a way of loving your neighbor as yourself. You recognize your own and your neighbor's worth simultaneously." As you become a miracle worker in the world, you realize that your own healing is directly related to the healing of those around you. Don't deprive the world of this gift. Stick around for the miracle.

Reflect and Recap

Each day offers you an opportunity to take inventory of your ego. The *Course* has a beautiful affirmation that inspires me to fearlessly look at my ego every day: "Above all else I want to see." A powerful suggestion I leave you with is to spend time each night looking at your ego's behavior throughout the day. My inventory practice is to write in my journal at the top of a page: "Above all else I want to see." Then I make a list of my ego's false perceptions throughout the day. With loving eyes I forgive my wrong-minded thoughts and actions, and I pray for release. This daily practice keeps me aware of my ego's patterns and supports my practice of inviting my ~*ing* in for healing. In an instant I release the fears of the day and clear my mind for happy dreams.

With your flashlight, chisel, and hammer, you will always be armed with the loving desire to grow beyond the ego's illusions. Use these tools each moment of your life and create subtle shifts for miraculous change.

MIRACLE MAINTENANCE TOOLKIT

Cracking open to your golden light is one thing, but nurturing your glow is another. To keep your inner light shining bright, you must be mindful of a few key miracle-minded practices. Outlined next are my best tactics for keeping your light shining bright.

Mind Your Own Practice

As a miracle worker in the world you must accept that you are not alone on this journey of new perceptions. Your neighbors, lovers, colleagues, friends, and enemies are all on the same radical road with you. Accepting miracles in your life requires that you be faithful to the practice in order to serve yourself and the world. Be mindful of the following principles as you carry the message of love into your life. Be diligent to keep your side of the street clean and mind your own practice.

Be Patient
The *Course* reminds us, "Infinite patience produces immediate results." Try not to get hung up about how and when miracles will occur. Trust that every simple shift toward love is a miracle. In each moment of stillness a new awakening occurs. My favorite message from the *Course* is, "Those who are certain of the outcome can afford to wait and wait without anxiety." Let these words grace your life with peace and patience. Trust and know that with love anything is possible. Be patient and expect miracles.

Seek to Find Joy in a Joyless Place

It's easy to be committed to love when everything is going great in our lives, or when we ignore the issues of the world. It's entirely different to be committed to love in the midst of dark periods or situations. A powerful way to work through these darker times is to stay committed to the *Course* practice of finding joy in a joyless place. In each instant you can remember love. You have the power to "turn an ancient hatred into a holy love." Throughout your life use the affirmation: "I seek to find joy in a joyless place." I encourage you to bring this affirmation into your regular practice, and you will become more comfortable seeking love than settling for fear.

Look at the Problem So It Can Be Solved

I've witnessed many people use their practice to spiritually bypass the issues of the world. It's easy to throw down affirmations and wave prayer flags, but it's much more difficult to acknowledge our discomfort as a spiritual assignment. The *Course* says, "Let me recognize the problem so it can be solved." Upon recognizing each of our problems as assignments to grow, we can be guided to perceive them differently. When "only love is real" is our mantra, we're not expected to ignore the fear of the world. Instead, we should use it as a learning device. Remember that "no one is sent to anyone by accident" and that every experience we have, if brought to our ~ing, will be a great assignment for spiritual growth. Accepting this truth will help you honor all your life's experiences, the good and the bad.

Don't Obey the Ego's Interpretation of Fear

Though the *Course* says not to deny your fear, it doesn't suggest that you obey your ego's interpretation of it. Acknowledging your ego's fear is much different from believing in it. So remember throughout your life that a primary goal when addressing fear is to be the gentle witness. You've begun to learn the practice of disobeying your ego's rules and choosing love instead. Always try your best not to obey your ego's interpretations.

Let Go of External Perceptions

As you deepen your miracle-minded practice you stop placing your happiness or sadness in external circumstances. Becoming a miracle worker leads to fulfillment, inspiration, and ease due to your spiritual connection to your ~*ing*. When you live in this way, you no longer look to outside circumstances to be your source of happiness. In addition, the outside circumstances that used to baffle you no longer have the same hold. You'll feel a sense of relief knowing that your external experience doesn't dictate your internal experience. As a loyal miracle worker, you no longer subscribe to the fundamental law of the ego, and your happiness doesn't rely on something outside of yourself.

Deny the Ego's Interpretation of the World

When your right mind sets in, you'll come to dissociate from your ego's perception of the world. Instead you'll witness the ego in action but remember that the false perceptions are not your truth. You will no longer feel a charge from the ego's projections;

instead you'll gently look upon them and unconsciously and intuitively call on another thought instead. It's wild to recognize
your new behavior!

Be Mindful Not to Make Your Practice Special

When you embark on a spiritual practice, there can be a ten-
dency to make yourself feel special for choosing love. The specialness you place upon yourself creates more separation from
others. Be mindful of how you may make your spiritual practice
special.

Learn the Happy Lessons of Forgiveness

Each moment of your life and each thought you have offer you
an opportunity to forgive. As you grow your practice, be conscious to call on the F word in all situations. Through forgiveness you will be released. Accepting that the world is a
classroom where you learn the happy lessons of forgiveness will
be your greatest gift on your path. Simply accept each encounter as an assignment and you will be released from the ego's
story. The *Course* teaches, "Perfect love casts out fear. If fear
exists there is no perfect love." Take this with you into all situations and whenever fear arises, ask yourself, "Where is the
love?" Then throw down an F bomb and forgive.

I hope these gentle reminders will act as a guide for you to become even more mindful of your ego as you strengthen your
miracle-minded practice. Often when people open up to this
type of work, they can feel scared by the ego. That reaction is

totally normal—after all, ego thoughts are scary. If your awareness of the ego becomes frightening in any way, make sure you
get back to basics. Remember that the ego is, as the *Course* says,
"vicious at best, suspicious at worst." Accepting that the ego's
tricks are part of the healing process will greatly soothe your
fear. Don't get freaked out by all that you witness. Simply use
the ego's daily craziness as new opportunities to surrender to
your ~*ing*.

Be Proud of Your Miracle-Worker Commitment

Something really amazing happens when you commit to a
spiritual practice: an internal shift occurs as a result of accepting your spiritual calling. Even if you don't see major external
shifts at first, you experience a sense of relief on the inside.
This relief is based on the fact that you've finally chosen the
peaceful path. Your commitment to love is the greatest gift
you'll ever give yourself and the world. The simple choice to
live a miraculous life is a powerful move into a whole new way
of existing. Be very proud of your dedication and willingness
to change.

As you embark on the rest of your life, bring this commitment with you. All you need is the willingness to choose love,
and the Universe will show you what to do. Keep your heart
and mind open to receive your ~*ing*'s direction and trust always
that the Universe has your back. Know that no matter how difficult the situation, there is always a spiritual solution. Remember that you don't need to seek the solution—the answer is in
you, and your internal teacher will always show you the way.

Stay faithful, willing, and receptive to love. Enjoy the miraculous journey of living a miraculous life.

> No course whose purpose is to teach you to remember what you really are could fail to emphasize that there can never be a difference in what you really are and what love is.
>
> —*A COURSE IN MIRACLES*

Acknowledgments

I begin by acknowledging YOU, my reader. Thank you for having the willingness to change, the openness to see a new perspective, and the intention to know more. Your desire to shift your perspective and experience miraculous change inspires me every day. Thank you.

I thank and honor the team who worked to create this book. My agent, Michele Martin. You are an angel guiding my literary path. I thank my editor, Gary Jansen, and the team at Crown for your support and faith in *May Cause Miracles*. I thank my PR team at Sarah Hall PR for creatively sharing this message with the world. Finally, with endless gratitude, I thank my copy editor, Katie Karlson, for your support and love for the work. Each word in this book has been blessed by you.

About the Author

New York Times bestselling Gabrielle Bernstein appears regularly as an expert on NBC's Today Show, has been featured on Oprah's Super Soul Sunday as a next-generation thought leader, and was named "a new role model" by the New York Times. She is also the author of the books Add More ~ing to Your Life, Spirit Junkie, and the forthcoming book Miracles Now (publishing in April 2014). Gabrielle is also the founder of HerFuture.com, a social-networking site for women to inspire, empower and connect. Her personal website is Gabbyb.tv.

Gabrielle Bernstein is available for select readings and lectures. To inquire about a possible appearance, please contact the Random House Speakers Bureau at rhspeakers@randomhouse.com or 212-572-2013.